Carina

Carina

A Story of Hope and Healing

by
Laura Eastman Malcolm

Cover design and chapter icons by Max Horton

Chapter One

The golden palette of the setting sun bathed the most idyllic view of the city of Florence. The light dappling the city was tranquil and yet pulsating with life. The citizens of Florence bustled about, preparing to retire for a harmonious evening with their families. As night descended all became velvet darkness. Only the cupola of the Duomo Cathedral gleamed as it guarded its precious ward, magnificent Florence.

Suddenly a chilling sound shattered the night. A woman's cries were heard coming from a noble family's palazzo. "Help me! Please, God, help me!"

The foremost reigning noble family of the Principality of Tuscany had been waiting anxiously for the Duchess Grazia to give birth to an heir. She had had a difficult pregnancy, and she unexpectedly entered into labor a month early. Her husband, Duke Onorio, had departed that morning to give attention to duties in Urbino. However, because of this urgent development, a messenger on horseback was dispatched to call the Duke to return to Florence as soon as possible.

The family's attendants and servants paced up and down the long, vaulted hallway outside the palazzo's birthing chamber, while inside the Duchess Lucrezia, Duke Onorio's mother, and Anna, Lucrezia's trusted handmaiden, attended to Grazia. The atmosphere in the room was laden with anxiety, as Grazia breathed with great difficulty.

Anna tried to soothe her, pressing cool linen compresses on her forehead as she coaxed her towards childbirth, saying, "Courage, dear Grazia, the babe is almost with us."

In her close to twenty years of service as maidservant to Lucrezia, this was Anna's most harrowing of nights. Although Anna was a midwife who had delivered many babies in the noble families of Florence, Duchess Grazia's problematic pregnancy created excruciating tension. She silently prayed for a boy, as she knew that a male heir would definitively secure a powerful position for Duchess Lucrezia in the Principality of Tuscany.

"How much longer?" Lucrezia questioned nervously.

"She is struggling, but I think it will be soon," Anna assured her.

Turning away from the bedside, Lucrezia flung open the door to the birthing chamber, hoping to find that her son Onorio had returned. With no sign of him, she ordered everyone to be dismissed from the crowded hallway to go down to the main banquet hall for the evening meal.

Lucrezia's finely chiseled features reflected the haughty breeding of centuries of Florentine nobility. A current reigning matriarchal noble, she had lost her husband to illness ten years previously. She sorely missed him, as her ruling position without him was challenging. At this time in history, Italy consisted of a series of principalities under submission to the Pope, known as papal states. Florence was the thriving capital of the Principality of Tuscany. Lucrezia's son, Duke Onorio, was an important nobleman, which added to her position as a powerful and influential woman.

Anna placed more compresses to soothe the Duchess Grazia. She tried to get her to sip an herbal potion to ease the pain, but Grazia, growing increasingly weak and pale, turned away and softly implored, "Lord, a healthy baby, please, that's all I ask. Please, Lord!"

Anna resumed her position at the foot of the bed to assist with the birth, but by now a growing sense of dread was filling the birthing chamber. She saw that a foot of the infant was coming down the birth canal first. The baby would be breech.

Grazia was bleeding profusely, and her face grew ashen. Her cries slowly subsided as the candles flickered. A hush came over the room. Lucrezia and Anna held their breath, frozen in a moment of stillness. Anna finally was able to extract the newborn infant. The room went silent. Grazia and the baby laid motionless.

Ecstatic at the birth of the child, Lucrezia demanded, "Is it a boy?"

At first Anna felt puffed up with pride at the successful birth of the babe. She quickly clamped and cut the umbilical cord and laid the still silent infant on the bed to turn her attention to the young duchess. Grazia was no longer breathing. "No," Anna whispered with increasing horror. She gently shook Grazia's lifeless form. "Grazia!" she pleaded.

Turning to Lucrezia to urge her to summon a doctor to the palazzo, she saw the duchess scrutinizing the baby. "There is something wrong with it."

Anna joined her, and the two women looked down at the infant, a girl. She looked hideously contorted, curled up into a tight C-like shape, with her head jammed between her legs and her knees stuck behind her ears. The newborn barely appeared to be breathing.

Unable to control herself, Lucrezia hissed, "God, why have you cursed my family with this deformed creature?" She glared down at the infant.

Anna grew terrified. Her position with Lucrezia had been one of privilege for a servant, and she was privy to Lucrezia's most intimate confidences. She had witnessed firsthand Lucrezia's mercurial and vindictive nature when she had blocked the hopes and advances of rival nobles, maintaining her position by maligning them. Lucrezia had trusted her to deliver a normal, healthy baby.

Grazia was dead, and Lucrezia did not have a male heir.

Hoping that something miraculous would occur, Anna started to clean the babe. She winced. The deformity was shocking, and she had yet to clearly see the babe's face.

"It would be better if you had died," she thought.

Lucrezia turned her back on the tragic scene and moved some distance away from the bed, covering her eyes with one hand and holding her stomach with the other hand. As if reading Anna's mind, she announced, "The child is dead. The Duchess Grazia shows no sign of life. Both Grazia and the child are dead!"

Anna looked at her in disbelief. Snapping to a straight and rigid stance, Lucrezia turned to face Anna and repeated her proclamation, "The child is dead!"

"But . . ." Anna stammered.

Lucrezia, with a murderous look, defied any objection. "Grazia was not capable, and frequently in pain during this pregnancy. We shall bury all of this along with Grazia. Unfortunately, she was not destined for a happy life."

"But . . . what about the babe?"

"The child is dead. Take it away." Lucrezia grabbed some linen cloths and shoved them into Anna's unwilling hands. "Now!"

Anna quickly wrapped up the baby. "What will you tell Duke Onorio? What will you tell the people?"

"The truth!" said Duchess Lucrezia. "The baby is dead. Grazia is dead. Go to your room and wrap the body for burial and bring it back here. Then I will make the announcement."

Clutching the baby, Anna exited the rear door of the birthing chamber and hastened through the corridors of the palazzo until she reached her room. Facing a heart-breaking and apparently unsolvable situation, she sank onto her bed. She shoved the bundled baby down a few feet away from her. The babe now was breathing with a rasping sound, an amorphous mass moving and poking inside the linens. Anna looked at the bundle with a glazed, detached expression. She wiped her hands on her skirts and brushed off her clothes, as if to disassociate herself from the babe. She knew what she had to do.

She rose to her feet, facing the baby, arching her head high and looking down at the thing laying before her. Stepping away, Anna reached for one of her bed pillows. She closed her eyes, turned her head away and slowly lowered the pillow over the infant. As the sound of the baby's breathing stilled and she felt it moving, Anna's breath came in shallow gulps and her heart beat wildly. At first, she pressed the pillow down hard with her own tearful babblings, broken by her panting. But finally, as she knelt beside the baby in tears, she released her pressure bearing down, and she backed away. "I'm sorry, I'm sorry."

Taking the pillow off the baby, Anna unwrapped the babe, and examined her closely. The baby was still alive and gulped quietly for air. Was this a blessing or a curse? Anna quieted down. She suddenly realized a way to appease both her conscience and Lucrezia. Anna grabbed her bed pillow and rolled it up to imitate the small shape and size of a newborn babe. She encased it in the linens Lucrezia had given her and tore the last one in strips that she used to secure the small bundle. This was the substitute for the babe and would be buried in Grazia's casket. She felt certain Lucrezia would not allow anyone to examine the infant.

Anna then disappeared into the deep recesses of her wardrobe closet where she rumbled and rustled about, making room for a small wooden chest of drawers which she maneuvered with difficulty from her bedchamber into the back corner of the wardrobe. No longer bewildered, Anna executed her moves swiftly and deftly. She swaddled the baby in one of her shawls. She then placed the baby in a drawer, stuffing the space with garments suited to muffle noise. But strangely the babe was still quiet and not crying.

She secured the closet door and stood in front of it, contemplating the effectiveness of her hiding and soundproofing the babe within. She then quickly opened the door again, burrowed her way back to the babe, and slightly pulled ajar the drawer to at least give her a chance of survival. She locked her bedchamber door from the outside, furtively glancing in every direction for observing eyes. With the substitute for the baby in her arms, she returned to the birthing chamber where Grazia lay dead and Lucrezia was waiting for her.

She knocked on the rear door of the birthing chamber. Without a word Lucrezia opened the door, grabbed the tiny bundle from Anna and closed the door. Anna caught her breath as she leaned against the wall in the back hallway and listened to Lucrezia's deceitful performance; the sobbing, the wailing. Lucrezia then opened the front door to the birthing chamber and ordered a guard to go to the banquet hall to announce the death of Duchess Grazia and the child. In that moment Anna felt a loathing for her mistress. Even though Anna had been privy to every outrageous plot within the ducal palazzo, this one now unfolding was the worst.

Anna returned to her bedroom and found the babe was still alive in the drawer in her closet. Anna became overcome with anxiety anew, herself out of breath and suddenly doubting her plan. Actually, she had no plan. She only had the thought that she had to get rid of the newborn babe in some way.

Anna prepared herself to leave the palazzo and scooped up the newborn duchess. Hoping to keep her quiet, Anna dipped a cloth in water by her bedside and immediately the babe started suckling. She loosened her own bodice and placed the babe against her chest and then covered herself with a heavy cloak for traveling.

News of the ducal family's tragedy spread rapidly throughout the palazzo and Anna passed servants in tears, others scurrying about with news of the impending funeral preparations. It was well after midnight, and Anna hurried to the stable and asked a palazzo guard to saddle her a horse. A woman riding a horse at night would have aroused suspicion, but with the palazzo in turmoil and Anna's clever story of having to inform Duchess Lucrezia's sister of the tragedy, her request was unchallenged.

It was a cloudless, full moon night as Anna slowly made her way with her bundle thrust into her dress bodice and hidden under her cloak. She headed across the Ponte Vecchio, moving away from the palazzo on the south side of the Arno river. As she passed through Piazza Santissima Annunziata it crossed Anna's mind to leave the babe on the doorstep of the Ospedale degli Innocenti, a convent dedicated to receiving orphaned children. But what if the nuns discovered the truth of the babe's birth? Wracked with fear, she could not follow through.

Anna continued heading toward the Florentine hills overlooking the city. She did not know if she could discern the babe breathing or not, the little bundle was so quiet. Florence was now behind her, the dawn not far off, and Anna still had no idea as to how she would dispose of the babe. She was not capable of just throwing her bundle into a roadside ditch and abandoning it.

The narrow road she followed eventually led her to the small town of Settignano, which overlooked Florence, and she realized she would be able to leave her 'parcel' by the central fountain in the town piazza. Surely someone would discover the babe. "God help whoever will," she prayed.

With the clatter of her horse's hooves on the cobblestones, Anna passed through the silent streets of Settignano. She rode directly into the middle of the piazza and stopped. She glanced around. She appeared to be the only person up at that hour. Unable to dismount, she carefully lowered her clandestine bundle to the ground with a slight thud, then turned her horse around and quickly rode off.

Chapter Two

It was still dark when the Maestro and his young Studio assistant, Pietro, loaded their paints and easels into the Maestro's horse drawn cart and made their way to the piazza in Settignano. Pietro set up the easels while the Maestro briefly dozed off. It was the day before Pietro's 10th birthday, and the Maestro had promised they would capture the golden hue of the sun as it rose over the eastern hills. Pietro could barely suppress his excitement at this opportunity to develop his painting skills. The first bird sang and then another and another. Pietro shook the Maestro's shoulder gently. "Maestro, wake up," he whispered, "The light is coming!"

But suddenly the sound of a horse's hooves pierced the dawn chorus of bird song, and Pietro caught a glimpse of a rider leaving the piazza. As the crest of the eastern hills turned golden, both men heard the muffled cry of an infant.

"Go see what is happening. Go!" the Maestro ordered Pietro.

Taken by surprise, Pietro carefully approached and knelt, peering at the linen wrapped bundle.

"Bring it here," called the Maestro.

Pietro hesitated and cautiously picked up the now squirming bundle. He held it at arms' length as he hurried back and thrust it into the Maestro's arms.

The Maestro gently removed a corner of the shawl to reveal a glimpse of a baby's face.

Understanding that the bundle was an infant, Pietro asked, "What should we do with it?"

The Maestro sighed deeply. He looked at the baby bundle. He looked at his canvas awaiting the first brushstroke. He looked up heavenward into the sky. He needed to pay attention to his work. Instead, he said, "Someone has to take this child home. It needs to be cared for, and it looks as though we've been chosen."

Pietro reluctantly peeked at the babe in the unfolding morning light and reeled back in protest. "Can't we leave it where we found it? Someone else will take care of it."

The Maestro shook his head.

Pietro interjected again. "I could chase down whomever left it here."

"Take the babe home immediately and give it to Lydia. She is a wet nurse and will know what to do. Then come back and get me and we will pack up and return home."

Pietro gingerly carried the bundle back on foot to the Maestro's home on the far edge of Settignano. Having to deliver the abandoned infant to Lydia rankled him. Pietro was the son of a Florentine well-to-do family of merchants and considered a child prodigy. His parents had consigned him to be tutored by the Maestro, the finest painter working in the Tuscan Principality and beyond. Even though Pietro had only been there three months, the Maestro had acknowledged his artistic capabilities, and he gave Pietro special attention. The eldest in his family, raised with many younger siblings whom he had always considered noisy, needy and bothersome, Pietro thrived on this attention. Spending hours in the Studio with the Maestro and his apprentices learning how to mix paint colors, draw and develop compositions felt like a marvelous privilege. But this morning had been ruined by the bundle in his arms. He intended to be rid of this thing as quickly as possible and hurry back to attend to the Maestro.

Chapter Three

Lydia had lit the magnificent fireplace in the Studio kitchen to provide warmth from the spring chill and was busy cleaning up and creating order in the Studio, sweeping under the easels while contemplating what she should prepare for the midday lunch. Since the young Pietro had come to the Studio, life had become somewhat topsy-turvy, and now the Maestro intended to teach Pietro about the importance of light. That's why he'd made the plan to go to the piazza before dawn to paint with the boy. To Lydia's mind what he needed was to be inspired to learn better manners and respect. Pietro was undoubtedly talented, but he was not easy to work with, and was often inconsiderate.

As if to confirm her thoughts, Lydia heard the front door swing open and Pietro barged into the Studio. He brusquely shoved his unwanted bundle, now squirming and whimpering, towards Lydia. Totally surprised, Lydia accepted the bundle and immediately recognized the soft pulse of life of an infant in her arms.

"Where did you . . .?"

"In the piazza — someone on horseback just dumped it there and then the Maestro insisted I retrieve it and give it to you."

"Someone just abandoned . . ." Her sentence trailed off as Pietro turned on his heels and with great irritation marched out of the Studio to return to the Maestro.

Lydia held the tiny babe close to her chest, and gently swayed back and forth as she made her way to her bedroom behind the kitchen. She shut the door and laid the baby on the bed, and warily unwrapped the shawl. She immediately noted the unnatural look of the infant's body and the tangle of limbs. The child was strangely deformed. It was as if her body was folded in half. Some of the umbilical cord was still attached, and the babe had not even been cleaned after birth. Lydia wondered how this tiny creature could be alive. But the baby was breathing, and, amazingly, not crying, perhaps because it didn't have enough strength to lament. Her astonishment at the babe's misshapen form soon melted into compassion, and she cleaned the infant. Being a wet nurse, Lydia lifted the infant to her breast and let her suckle. A quiet peace came over both of them.

Sitting on her bed with the babe in her arms and nursing, she wondered where the child came from. Who were her parents? She could imagine a mother's dismay at giving birth to such an infant. Was she overwhelmed at the notion of looking after such a child? Pietro said a stranger on horseback had dumped the babe in the town piazza. But to be abandoned like that? To be separated from her family? As Lydia pondered this, memories from her own stillborn childbirth came flooding back.

Before working for the Maestro, Lydia had been the maid for the Duchess Gentile of Florence, who had commissioned the Maestro to paint her portrait. While serving in the Duchess's household, Lydia had secretly and mistakenly become pregnant, and her child died at birth. It happened that the Duchess had also given birth a few months previously and wanted a wet nurse to help her feed her baby so she could get back to her activities and duties as a member of the Florentine nobility. The transition was effortless, and Lydia nurtured the Duchess's baby, and thus was able to avoid a scandal in the Duchess's household. When the Duchess began sitting for her portrait, Lydia would attend the Duchess with her baby at the Maestro's Studio. While the infant slept, Lydia often busied herself with the Maestro's household maintenance needs. In time the Maestro got to know and appreciate Lydia's management skills, and when the Duchess's babe no longer needed to be nursed, he invited Lydia, with the Duchess Gentile's approval, to transfer to his household to work for him. Lydia gratefully accepted, as she was able to turn her back on the pain of her previous history. Although the Maestro had been married, his wife had succumbed to illness at a young age, and thus he was always in need of servant help for his home and the Studio entourage of students. Within the year, Lydia gained his trust and became the manager of his household affairs.

Other noblewomen who wanted to be free from breastfeeding their babies soon heard about Lydia's presence at the Maestro's Studio. Lydia continued as a wet nurse while working her household duties for the Maestro, and this was a welcome added income for her.

Now as Lydia gazed down at the deformed orphaned newborn in her arms, her heart melted with an array of emotions. She pondered what might have happened to her own child, had she not died at birth. With compassion in her heart, Lydia fondled the babe's head and spoke tenderly to her. "Poverina." As if in response, the baby opened her blue eyes, and it seemed to Lydia that she gazed into the depths of Lydia's soul. When the baby fell into a deep sleep, Lydia improvised a cradle by removing a drawer from the small trunk in the corner of her bedroom, and brought the babe into the kitchen where it was warmer.

Lydia stoked the huge hearth in the kitchen and began to prepare a meal for the Maestro and Pietro. She found herself moving slowly, quite befuddled by the events of the day.

Within the hour she heard Samuele, the old stable hand, welcoming them home. Pietro came into the kitchen, complaining that he had met the Maestro when was already returning home in the horse-drawn cart, having packed up the easels and paints by himself. "He told me he couldn't concentrate on his work and had to come find out if you had been able to nurse the baby."

Usually, welcoming the Maestro home was one of Lydia's favorite moments of the day, because his presence gave an assurance of stability and order. But today felt different.

"Lydia, tell me what is happening. Is the baby going to survive?" the Maestro asked as he entered the kitchen.

"Right now she is asleep. I was able to nurse her, and she is swaddled and resting here by the hearth." Then Lydia said softly, "But she is strangely deformed, and I don't know if she will live."

"Can you bring her into the Studio so I can see her?" asked the Maestro. He turned to go and sit in his armchair next to the fireplace in the Studio. Although only in middle age, the Maestro looked wizened due to his beard and abundance of shoulder length hair sprinkled with grey. Having lost his wife to illness in his earlier years, and being without children, he was touched by the idea of caring for the baby.

Lydia gathered up the infant, who had been sleeping peacefully in the make-shift cradle. She carefully carried the orphaned babe into the Studio and gently placed her in the lap of the Maestro. The babe awakened and stirred and once again opened her blue eyes. Lydia watched as the Maestro tenderly caressed her head, as if his hands could impart healing to her.

Lydia suddenly felt like she was sinking. "Can't we take her to the nuns at the Innocenti? They will take care of her, and she will be amongst other unfortunates. Perhaps that is best."

The Maestro quietly shifted his gaze from the baby in his lap to Lydia. "Lydia, we can only receive this child into our home if you also give your approval and loving support."

There was a pause as Lydia lowered her eyes in thought. Then she raised her head with a fixed gaze from the babe to the Maestro. She remembered her own lost child.

"It is in God's hands and ours," offered the Maestro, speaking with great loving kindness.

Lydia took the babe from the Maestro's lap into her arms and cradled her, swaying gently back and forth. She took in a deep breath as a tenderness of heart welled up inside her. "Yes," she said, weakly at first. "Yes, Maestro, she has come into our hands and hopefully into our hearts. Yes, may she survive and be blessed."

The Maestro sighed with relief. "Carina, Carina, my dear little one. Welcome to our home, and may the Lord God bless you with health and happiness as we commit to care for you."

As Lydia listened, transfixed, the Maestro's words were like sweet perfume, giving her hope. In her heart she joined the Maestro in his promise to care for tiny Carina. As if in recognition of the Maestro's words, the infant made a soft gurgling sound of happiness. Yes, Lydia was sure of it.

Chapter Four

Those first months with the presence of the baby required a big adjustment in the life of the Studio. The foremost concern was to see if she could survive. Lydia now had Carina to attend to in addition to her load of housework. But Lydia cherished and nurtured Carina to the best of her ability, and much to Lydia's surprise, Carina was thriving. Doctor Benedetto, a friend of the Maestro's, had examined her and declared that though she was frail and underweight, she seemed reasonably healthy, all things considered. It was clear that she had moments of pain, probably due to her deformed shape, and yet, she did not wail. Lydia or the Maestro would hold her up against their bodies and cradle her so she could absorb warmth and healing from them, and thus soothe her.

It was as if Carina understood that her new home was a place of calm and quiet, a refuge, and with every breath she took, she inhaled love. As Lydia nursed Carina, she whispered words of comfort. "I am caring for you, my child. Rest and be at peace." These very words ministered also to Lydia, as if they had come to her by divine means, to comfort her as well.

Lydia and the Maestro were increasingly entranced by her angelic countenance, her gurgling laugh. The Maestro's students too were taken by her; one brought her a new blanket, another a sculpted toy. Only Pietro remained somewhat indifferent towards Carina. He continued to show extraordinary artistic talent as a painter, and the Maestro gave him the responsibility to instruct the other students.

By the time Carina was a little over a year old she was crawling around the Studio, but at such a severe angle that she often knocked into things and bruised herself. This distressed Lydia immensely. Lydia painstakingly fed Carina until she could eventually feed herself, though it was with some difficulty. The Maestro fashioned a specially designed chair for Carina so she could slide up to the table and feed herself with her legs drawn up under the table. The Studio remained a place of utmost fascination for her, and with the Maestro's gentle guidance she learned to leave the art supplies alone. When she sat in the Maestro's lap, he noted how she seemed fascinated by the portraits on the easels. She gurgled with joy and laughed as if she wanted to befriend these special people being depicted.

As the Maestro and Lydia were active members of the parish community in Settignano, Carina became well known. A nun in the parish, Sister Clara, who was an expert in sewing handiwork and embroidery, made clothing for Carina which adhered to her shape. Each Sunday the Maestro and Lydia carried Carina to the Sunday Mass. Most members of the parish looked kindly towards little Carina, but some, perplexed by her strange shape, held themselves back out of fear.

When Lydia wasn't busy with the maintenance of the Maestro's home, she continued to dedicate her time to caring for Carina. She had become the substitute for Lydia's own lost child. Even Carina's deformed shape and mysterious family origin reminded Lydia of her own mishandled and unfortunate familial history.

But Lydia worried about Carina's future. Occasionally the Maestro grasped Carina's hands and tried to get her to stand, but she would gasp in pain and crumple, over and over, to Lydia's deep concern. Eventually Carina began to walk on her own, bent over, often using her hands on the ground or a nearby chair or wall to steady herself. To everyone's great happiness Carina began to speak normally, with keen understanding. Lydia became "Lee-Lee," and the Maestro became "My-My." What a delight for the Maestro and Lydia!

When Carina was about two years old, Lydia shared with the Maestro her fear. "Dear Maestro, what will the future of Carina be? What will happen to her when we are too old to take care of her? And when we pass away, what then?" Torn between her love for Carina and her dread of not being able to care for her, Lydia continued, "Should we not reconsider taking her to the nuns at the Innocenti convent in Florence? They will always be able to take care of her and protect her." The Maestro understood Lydia's fears, but he was committed to Carina, and she had a hold on his heart. The Maestro studied the holy Bible scriptures, and already much of the Bible was being translated from Latin into the Italian vernacular. The Maestro chose Psalm 146, verse 9, to pray and speak over Carina so as to bless her: "The Lord is good to everyone. He showers compassion on all his creation." He then suggested that they once again seek the medical counsel of Doctor Benedetto.

The Maestro called for Samuele and told him to go with the horse and cart to find the doctor at his home in the hills outside Settignano, a letter in hand from the Maestro.

To the Maestro's delight, Doctor Benedetto returned immediately with Samuele. He was pleasantly surprised when he saw the happy toddler, even though Carina was still bent over and had great difficulty maneuvering. Doctor Benedetto took Carina, along with Lydia, into their bedroom to give Carina a thorough examination, testing her reflexes. After examining her, he encouraged the Maestro and Lydia to wait patiently to see if she would grow and flourish. "Take it one day at a time. She is amazingly healthy. Let's hope she continues to eat well and develop physically. I cannot tell if this will be a lasting disability or if she can be treated with various therapies when she gets older."

Considering that it was already late morning, the Maestro invited Doctor Benedetto to remain for lunch, and while Lydia prepared, they retired to converse in the Maestro's private office in the Studio. The idea of some kind of therapy for Carina fascinated the Maestro, and he asked the doctor for ideas concerning the kind of apparatus which would need to be developed. The Maestro also shared with the doctor that he intended to teach Carina to read and write as a way of helping her develop the tools needed to navigate her life. When he questioned him about the reality of this possibility, Doctor Benedetto again assured the Maestro that his examination of Carina revealed that she was cognitively adept and not mentally injured by her unfortunate birth conditions. They would need to wait, however, to see if she would be able to integrate well into the household and develop good speech and then reading capability. "All with hope and prayers," the Maestro concluded.

The Maestro then gave Doctor Benedetto a tour of the Studio. While he was admiring all the artwork in progress, the distant sound of the church bells of the Duomo in Florence rang, communicating an important event. Pietro then arrived, and they asked him if he knew what the unusual tolling of the Duomo bells was about. "On my way to come here, I met my mother in Piazza Annunziata, and she shared that Duchess Lucrezia's daughter-in-law has given birth to an heir for her family."

"This would be an important and joyous event for Florence, so perhaps the bells communicate that," said the Maestro.

Indeed, the moment had arrived that Duchess Lucrezia had been waiting for. Duchess Francesca, the wife of her second son, Duke Eduardo, had successfully given birth to a baby heiress. Anna was present, but the responsibility for the birth had been given to a trusted family doctor. Lucrezia had hoped for a boy, but she was overjoyed with a healthy baby girl, and the little duchess was named Donatella, meaning "gift."

The birth of Donatella gave Lucrezia cause to ponder the unfortunate birth and death of Duchess Grazia and her baby. What a trauma that had been, and although Lucrezia tried to bury her memories and thoughts, she was still haunted by the horror of it all, including that fact that she favored her eldest son, Onorio, and would have preferred for him to produce an heir for the family.

Lucrezia asked Anna to summon Duke Onorio so he could congratulate his younger brother. Once he arrived, Duchess Lucrezia asked him to take a walk with her in the inner courtyard. This courtyard was one of the most formal gardens in all of Florence, and a protected place of privacy for Lucrezia's noble family. Doves fluttered under the eaves of the ducal palazzo and the sky was a brilliant blue. A somber Duke walked arm-in-arm with his mother.

Since the death of his beloved wife and the loss of their child he had been a pale shadow of his former self. This anguished Lucrezia. "My son, why don't you remarry? You are too solitary and lonesome, my dear. It would be good for you to have children. Eduardo's first child is born, and now you are no longer the source of our family's lineage. But if you remarry, this could change," Lucrezia said.

Shaking his head regretfully, the Duke replied, "Mother, I would most willingly oblige you, but my heart is still too troubled to think of marriage."

Chapter Five

The seasons passed and Lydia and the Maestro cared for Carina with loving attention. Doctor Benedetto gave Carina a yearly examination, approving of her development, but still not recommending a particular therapy until she reached a more advanced age. By the time Carina was four years old she moved with a lumbering walk, but with difficulty because her body continued to stoop, weighing down her head. She did not have the strength to stand upright, and it was painful when she tried. Lydia cut Carina's hair so that it would not fall into her face, leaving curly locks framing her beautiful countenance.

Although Carina's body continued to give her pain, she was blessed with a grateful outlook, and she always seemed keenly interested in all those around her. Carina often sought out Lydia or the Maestro. She would reach up and touch their cheek or lay a loving hand on their leg, always offering a smile. It was clear that Carina wanted to belong.

The Maestro and Lydia continued to take Carina with them to the Sunday Mass in Settignano. Although Carina did not understand the Latin Mass, and was too young to take communion, she loved being in the church with its music and rich candle-lit atmosphere.

One Sunday a new family in the village came to mass, accompanied by their three children. The girl, slightly older than Carina, had suffered an injury and walked with a severe limp. Carina immediately befriended her, boldly approaching her and asking her name. Even though the girl, whose face was also scarred, was reticent, Carina persisted. Soon Carina was engaging Sara in conversation, smiling every time she saw her new friend.

This opened Carina to the suffering in the world around her, and she was forever asking Lydia for something to give to the beggar who hobbled to the piazza every day. When Lydia realized that Carina had begun setting aside parts of her meals to give to the beggar and to an older woman in need, Lydia tried to intervene. But Carina could not be swayed. And so Lydia learned to make a little extra for those in need, always distributed by Carina. She even persuaded their neighbor, Signor Tommaso, to let Carina gather and distribute the fallen fruit from his plum tree, which leaned over onto the Maestro's property.

The Studio remained a sanctuary for Carina. She conversed with the students who befriended her and received her complimentary observations of their artwork. When she was seven years old, the Maestro began to use Carina as a model for his paintings, setting her in poses to highlight her cherubic face. The first of these paintings was a scene of Jesus healing the leper, and it sold immediately. Sensitive to Carina's struggles and aware of how painful it was for Carina to stay still in a position for modeling, he limited his requests that she pose. But it also gave her and the Maestro the opportunity for many hours of quiet conversation.

He hadn't forgotten his commitment to give Carina an education, and for the first few years he shared stories from the Bible with her. Carina was curious about his youth, so he also told stories about growing up in his family who owned a marble quarry outside Settignano. It was assumed that the

Maestro and his brothers would work with the family in the quarry, but their life was tough, and they were always covered with fine marble dust. The Maestro recounted how from a very young age he showed talent for drawing, and he continually asking for colored pencils and paints to adorn his sketches. His family wanted to apprentice him to a sculptor's studio in Florence to whom they provided the marble pieces, but the Maestro begged over and over to be apprenticed to a painter. Finally, they relented, and he joined a studio in Florence where various painters trained young developing artists.

Life was not all joy for Carina as she grew, and she continued lumbering with difficulty around the Studio. The Maestro designed a contraption with rollers for Carina to push and lean on to help her walk, but Carina banged into so many obstacles that it became a hazard. She reverted to walking bent over on her own, often using her hands on the ground to give her momentum and balance. Lydia would scold her when she did that. "Carina, stop that! You are not a monkey. Using your hands on the floor to 'walk' is not sanitary."

"I've never seen a monkey," said Carina.

"Never mind," Lydia replied. "I am just praying that you develop into a beautiful young lady."

"Well," Carina replied, now a precocious and witty eight-year-old and becoming more versed in scripture, "the Maestro always says that 'the fervent prayer of a righteous man avails much!'"

"So be it!" responded Lydia.

Lydia and Carina had a good laugh, and such was life at the Studio.

The Maestro sculpted and painted a walking stick for Carina, perfect for her height. He called it her "Psalm 23 staff," referring to a psalm that gave him great comfort:

> The LORD is my shepherd; I shall not want.
> For thou art with me; thy rod and thy staff,
> > they comfort me.

Carina wanted to help Lydia in the kitchen as best she could, and by the time she was nine years old she took responsibility for various chores to relieve Lydia of her workload. The Maestro made a short-handled broom for Carina, and she willingly swept the kitchen floor after their meals. She gathered vegetables from the garden when Lydia needed them and did her best to wash and clean them.

One Sunday after Mass, she approached Lydia and the Maestro, and with a smile asked if she could invite one of her beleaguered friends from church to join them for their Sunday lunch. Seeing the joy that Carina brought into the hearts of others, the Maestro and Lydia wondered why they had not extended this invitation earlier. They agreed that Carina could invite some of her needy friends for lunch every Sunday.

Inspired by the Maestro's love of beauty, Carina cultivated a flower garden, harvesting and planting seeds from the abundance of wildflowers nearby. She made bouquets of flowers from her garden and gave them to Lydia and the Maestro. She also carried her flower bouquets to adorn the church for the Mass on Sunday as an added touch of beauty, and would also give her bouquets to Sister Clara.

Sister Clara was well-educated and had a particular love and sensitivity for Carina. Seeing how his young ward was flourishing, the Maestro asked her to help with Carina's education. When Carina questioned whether she should be spending time on studies when it took away from the time she could devote to helping Lydia, the Maestro assured Carina it was her right. Boys and girls of noble birth were being educated in Florence. Why shouldn't she have the same opportunities? Sister Clara came once a week to the house, and Carina quietly studied with her in Lydia's bedroom. Sister Clara taught her the ABCs of writing and gave Carina exercises to do on her own. For reading material, Sister Clara used whatever vernacular translations of the Holy Bible were available, and Carina particularly loved learning about the healing miracles of Jesus's ministry.

About this time, one of the parish's dogs had a litter of pups, and Sister Clara had the idea to gift Carina with two of the pups so that she would have company and learn to care for others. At first the Maestro and Lydia objected, but Carina begged to adopt the puppies. She asked them first thing in the morning and right before she went to sleep with such fervor that they relented. Buono and Buona, as Carina named them, were added to the Studio family. The puppies stayed outside during the day, keeping Carina company as she tended to the vegetable garden and developed her flower garden, sometimes wreaking havoc. Lydia often heard cries of dismay and then laughter coming from the garden. Carina learned to cook meals for her two rascally pups with the help of Lydia's contributions from the Studio larder, and at night she would bring them into the kitchen so that they could be warm and safe. And so, Carina and her puppies grew, and life at the Studio proceeded harmoniously.

Chapter Six

The sleeping dogs lay sprawled in front of the Maestro's kitchen hearth as the dawn light crept over them. Hissing embers from the previous night's fire spat fitfully. Lydia had awakened, as was often the case, to find Carina missing from her little bed. Emerging from the bedroom to commence the daily household chores, Lydia's stomping around the kitchen disturbed the dogs. But what was that arm sticking out in a yawning gesture from amidst the dozing dogs? What was that brown-garbed form and that clump of curls? Twelve-year-old Carina rubbed her eyes and massaged her back, attempting to get her tightly-curled-up body, always pained in some way, to become limber enough to uncurl and arise.

Lydia made her way past the dogs surrounding Carina to begin fretting the fire's coals with a poker to bring up enough flames to encourage fresh logs to burn. The dogs and Carina stretched and yawned and shook themselves, appearing as one mass coming awake together.

"Time to rise," cajoled Lydia.

"Good morning, dear Lydia," Carina said with another yawn.

Lydia responded, "I'll believe you when you get up on your feet."

Carina smiled up at Lydia as she continued to massage her back, the dogs rubbing up against her. This morning game of "stretch-and-roll" always followed those nights when Carina crawled into their midst to bury herself amongst them, seeking their body warmth like hot water bottles to soothe her aching body.

Lydia piled logs onto the fire, and they caught flame, bringing life to the cavernous kitchen which would soon be filled with the aroma of coffee and breakfast. Carina rolled onto her knees, bent over with her forehead on the floor, her curly locks hiding her face. She whispered quietly to herself. Attempting to sit up, she appeared like a phoenix rising slowly amongst the dogs now wagging their tails.

"Need some help?" asked Lydia as she towered above the ragtag group.

"No, thanks, I have plenty of help," said Carina, turning her head to gaze heavenward.

Lydia disappeared into their bedroom and reemerged into the kitchen with Carina's walking staff. As she extended the staff to Carina she said, "If you mean those dogs, my dear, they may keep you warm through the night, but they won't help get you on your feet. And you shouldn't be sleeping with them anyway. They are dirty!"

"That's not what I mean."

Lydia, watching Carina rise to her feet, stooped over as ever, asked, "What DO you mean?"

Carina paused and cocked her head to one side to look up at Lydia with her beautiful face, encircled by honey-colored curls, and her huge sensitive eyes. Carina smiled knowingly, as if she were harboring a cherished secret. "I have very special angelic help."

Lydia extended a hand to Carina.

"If I didn't have special help, I wouldn't have made it this far," Carina said. "Of course, I am ever grateful to you and the Maestro."

Affectionately, Lydia offered, "Well, love, you just keep thinking that way, because it's a miracle that you can function at all." As Lydia gestured to a small bowl, she continued, "I need some berries from the garden for the Maestro's breakfast, so please get me some, all right? I know this is usually his one day of rest, but today is a very special day with the Festival of San Giovanni Battista. He needs to make his appearance at the Duomo Cathedral in Florence and then move on to the palazzo. As you know, the Maestro is invited for the celebration."

Lydia set about making breakfast, shaking her head and muttering to herself while slicing the previous day's baked bread and preparing a pot of water to boil eggs.

Carina took her first few steps of the day. She steadied herself, clinging to her walking staff, and shuffled about, petting the dogs as she passed by, singing a song of thanksgiving that had come to her that morning. Carina was weak in her flesh, but strong in her spirit.

After letting the dogs outside, she went out to pick the berries, and then brought them into the kitchen. She then disappeared into the bedroom she shared with Lydia to wash her face and get dressed before eating her breakfast with Lydia.

Carina usually started on her list of daily chores right after breakfast, but today was an exception, as she and Lydia would accompany the Maestro into Florence to attend the Mass in the Duomo Cathedral.

After finishing breakfast, Carina made her way slowly into the Studio, which was blanketed in a peaceful hush. As much as she loved the Studio when it was humming with life, she also appreciated the quietude of a Sunday morning when diffused light from the early morning sun streamed in through the large windows, creating various shapes like a wonderfully composed painting. Carina paused for a moment as a persistent scratching sound caught her attention. She made her way through the maze of art paraphernalia to find the Maestro sitting in his painter's chair, busily making charcoal sketches of a man's head from memory. "Maestro, good morning! You are up early."

The Maestro ceased his drawing, squinting at his work, displeased, and answered, "I couldn't sleep." Indicating his subject matter he said, "See this man? I was thinking about him all night. He is a villain and a scoundrel and my enemy! He is jealous of my artistry and tries to steal my commissions. With all the competition, treachery and conflicts always warring in Florence, I choose to live a peaceful life up here in Settignano. But evil attempts to seek me out to rob and destroy. But by the grace of God, Carina, evil will not succeed."

The Maestro placed his sketch on a nearby stand and motioned for Carina to come close to him. He helped her raise her upper body, positioning her so that she could see well. They assessed his drawing together.

"I'm surprised that you would spend your time making sketches of a man so . . ." Choosing her words carefully, she said, ". . . unworthy and wretched."

"I will use his face to contrast something of great beauty."

Carina said, "I didn't think you drew ugly subjects."

Although the Maestro regularly used Carina as a model due to the beauty of her face, the Maestro realized that Carina was indirectly referring to herself. "Actually, he is a handsome evildoer. It is what is inside that makes him ugly," the Maestro said.

Carina turned to face him, and he continued, "My beloved Carina, it is what's inside that makes you beautiful or ugly. We all have inner gifts that nourish us and can make us extraordinary. You have them, my dear, as do I. We have the assignment of discovering our divine inner gifts and developing them and using them to bless others."

Carina began to play with the beautifully embroidered and beaded collar of the Maestro's morning-robe. The violet and emerald-colored beads caught the light and sparkled, delighting her as she basked in the Maestro's edifying words. She listened intently and relished this moment alone with him. "How?" she asked.

"By the grace of God, you can use your inner gifts to become who you are meant to be in this life. And you have so much to share, my dearest. In fact, I have been hearing you singing lovely little songs that you have composed. Did you know you were a poet and a musician?"

"No!" said Carina with modesty. "But when you read the Psalms to me, I often hear about singing praises to the Lord, and it makes me want to do that too!"

"Aha!" exclaimed the Maestro. "Did you know that King David, who wrote many of the Psalms, was originally a shepherd boy who played beautifully on a simple 4-stringed instrument?"

"Oh, I would love to do that!"

"Well then," proclaimed the Maestro, "I will construct a musical instrument for you, and you can become a musician!" The idea of introducing a musical instrument into the life of the Studio inspired the Maestro, as he thrived on beauty and harmony.

Their peaceful and intimate moment was broken by the intrusion of Pietro, who normally did not come to work at the Studio on Sunday. Now a tall, handsome young man in his early twenties, he greeted the Maestro with great respect. "Good morning, Maestro. It's a beautiful day and the city of Florence is already astir and filling up with the crowds to celebrate the Festival of San Giovanni."

Pietro ignored Carina as was usual, and when Lydia arrived with the Maestro's breakfast tray, Pietro took the tray from her, and turning to the Maestro, he announced he would take the tray to the Maestro's quarters so he could eat in peace. When Lydia objected, Pietro demanded that Lydia, ten years his senior, also bring him his breakfast in the Maestro's room.

"And what's so special about you that you can't eat in the kitchen like every other day?" Lydia snapped. She shook her head in frustration and cast a furious look at the Maestro.

Shaken by any discord, Carina slipped away from the Maestro to distance herself from Pietro and Lydia.

"Come now, Pietro," the Maestro intervened, "where is your nobility of heart? Not to mention good manners! But even without the manners, we need to cherish one another and be sensitive to each other's needs. Beloved, please establish harmony between yourselves."

As always, the Maestro confirmed himself as the anchor in the Studio, the stalwart peacemaker who combined artistic genius with real spiritual understanding.

Returning the tone of conversation from the lofty to the mundane, Lydia reminded the Maestro that today he must dress properly for the Mass at the Duomo and to be particularly presentable when he dined at the palazzo after the service. The financial success of the Studio mattered to Lydia, with the Maestro providing for her and Carina, and she was always promoting good relationships between the Maestro and his patrons.

"You too!" she called out after Pietro as he followed the Maestro. She rattled off instructions as to how he was to conduct himself with the Maestro in the presence of the noble family. Pietro chose to ignore her, but Lydia was pleased to have the last word.

Chapter Seven

While the Maestro dressed and Lydia put all in order, Carina struggled on her own to prepare a huge cauldron of soup which would be left to bubble on the hearth while they were out. She reminded Lydia of the soup and its purpose, wanting to know if Lydia had any extra provisions in the larder to enrich its meager ingredients. Finding some rice for her, Lydia then went to her bedroom to pretty herself, leaving Carina to create her beggars' broth. It had become her custom every Sunday to invite whatever maimed, downtrodden and outcast friends she knew to come share the midday meal in the kitchen of the Maestro's Studio. Her weekly Sunday "beggars' banquet" was the highlight of her life and had caused the Maestro to don her with the affectionate title, "Our Lady of the Outcasts."

Alone in the kitchen, Carina tended to the difficult task of drawing water for the cauldron and cutting up the vegetables she had managed to gather from her garden. While waiting for the broth to boil she sang a joyful melody in anticipation of the afternoon fête, dreaming of the musical instrument that the Maestro had promised to make her.

Soon Samuele arrived on his horse, Golden Slippers, to hitch up the horse-drawn wagon, and Lydia reappeared with a pretty shawl for Carina to wear, and there was the Maestro looking so distinguished in his artistically embroidered cloak. Samuele and Lydia helped Carina to get up and situated into their cart. Although awkward and difficult for

Carina, off they all went, accompanied by Pietro following on his horse, to participate in the great celebration at the Duomo. As they descended the hillside from Settignano towards Florence, others heading into the city flowed onto the road. Upon arriving in Florence, Samuele found a good place to tie up the horse and cart in Piazza San Marco, and their little group proceeded on foot towards the center of the city.

Lydia stayed close to help Carina as it was a struggle for her to keep up, and the gathering crowd of people often caused her to cling close to the walls of the narrow streets. As they moved forward Carina twisted her head to look upward and caught glimpses of the Duomo, the magnificent cathedral that dominated the heart of the city with its towering, dome-shaped cupola, also known as "the vault of heaven." The Maestro was considerate, stopping and waiting for Carina and Lydia to catch up. But if it had been up to Pietro, dressed in his finest, they would have outpaced the women and left them far behind. Noting his annoyed expression, Carina wondered why Pietro had stubbornly refused to adopt the virtue of humility that was a main focus in the Maestro's teaching. How could he not see that his outstanding creative talent could be used to communicate beauty, that his paintings were capable of giving joy, that they could transform those who admired them rather than simply proving that he was an artistic genius?

Suddenly there was a stir in the crowd as the noble family and their entourage of guards approached. The crowd parted and pulled back, pressing up against the walls of the narrow street's buildings to let the carriages and guards on horseback pass through on their way to the Duomo. Facing the building façade, Carina used her hands to pull herself up, clinging to the huge wall stones for support to avoid the crush. She managed to turn her head as the decorated carriage passed inches away from her. Inside sat a girl close to her age, with the fieriest, reddest hair Carina had ever seen. She stared briefly at Carina, her eyes a clear blue, and then turned to say something to a haughty older woman who stared straight ahead with an expression of pride.

"Who was that girl with the red hair?" Carina asked Lydia when the last of the carriages passed by.

"That is the young Duchess Donatella, the granddaughter of the woman beside her, who is the Duchess Lucrezia. And those must be other members of the noble family with her."

The crowd followed the noble family up the steps into the Duomo, and Lydia and Carina fell behind the Maestro and Pietro. Inside the Duomo, the Maestro and Pietro were ushered to a more prominent position close to the noble entourage, while Lydia and Carina remained in the back. Many of the residents in Settignano had come to know and love Carina, but here in this magnificent city she felt self-conscious. Even though she loved being in church, with Lydia's approval she disappeared today out the Duomo's side entrance door, as she was on a special mission. On the Festival of San Giovanni Battista, and other holidays when the Maestro and his Studio family attended Mass in Florence, Carina always made a visit to the bell tower to visit Adamo, the belfry man who rang the Duomo's famous resonate bells in Giotto's bell tower. An outcast like herself, Adamo was an odd, lonely little runt of a man, living only to ring the church bells. Carina had befriended him several years ago, her only Florentine friend, and now he anticipated this cherished visit from her. Lumbering up the steps to the top of the bell tower, Carina greeted Adamo affectionately. She presented him with a little package of extra berries she had picked that morning and had managed to carefully protect in her garment. Grateful for her thoughtfulness, Adamo had done likewise by prearranging for his father, the town baker, to save some of the day's festival pastries to give to Carina for her special weekly lunch gathering at the Studio. Adamo attended when he could, along with her other rejected and downtrodden friends. Carina was delighted and told him she hoped he would be able to come later to Settignano for her beggar's banquet.

Adamo's family bakery was not far from the Duomo. After saying her goodbye, Carina clumsily trundled her way from the bell tower to the Arno river and up to the back steps of the bakery where Adamo's father waited for her. He presented her with a sack of delicious breads and pastries which he knew Carina's guests would love. The baker reached down through Carina's curls to lift her little chin so he could see her beautiful, thankful face. He reminded her that she was always welcome to come to receive his bakery's delicacies for her precious friends and thanked her for the friendship she offered his son.

Carina carried the carefully packed breads and pastries as she moved with difficulty along the banks of the Arno river. Due to her posture, she was only partially able to enjoy the splendor of Florence on this glorious day. And what a gracious city it was, with its artfully crafted buildings, decorated with a symmetry of granites and marbles. Even the inhabitants' clothing created a flow of color that melded with the architecture, the river, and the sky into a mellifluous harmony. In sharp contrast to this felicitous atmosphere were the few passersby who jeered at Carina, stepping aside so as not to be close to her.

Carina passed a few bridges before she stopped in an area of the exposed riverbank abloom with flowers. As her parcel was too cumbersome to carry down the bridge's steps, Carina hid it as well as she was able on top of the stairs and scrambled down to the river to gather the flowers she cherished as decoration for her Sunday lunch. With some of the flowers Carina intended to weave a garland for Lydia. The fragrance of the flowers and the gentle flow of the river filled her with happiness. Carina lifted up Lydia and the Maestro and her precious, outcast acquaintances to God, calling upon the Lord to bless them.

The sound of a group of ruffians coming across the Ponte alle Grazie above Carina broke the peace. One of them was carrying a big sack of peaches on his back, and their conversation revealed that they had stolen them from a fruit and vegetable vendor at the nearby Porcellino market. They were alternately taking gulps from a bottle of wine that they passed amongst the five of them. When the rowdies spotted Carina's package of breads and pastries, they pounced on it gleefully and picked out the choicest morsels and stuffed their mouths. One of the gang soon spotted Carina on the riverbank below as she vainly tried to see what was unfolding. Not appreciating the precious nature of this bundle of treats for Carina, he picked up a special bread and catapulted it at Carina. It missed her and the bread ended up floating in the river. The rest of the devils delighted at this mean fun and joined in the game of aiming shots in the form of pastries at Carina, ignoring her muffled cries. Coming to the end of the bakery-booty, and not wanting to discontinue their cruel game, the boys realized that they had more ammunition in their sack of peaches. The rapscallions threw some of their plunder at Carina, several hitting her hard. The pitiful sight of Carina watching her bread and pastries floating down the Arno river did little to temper their cruelty.

Carina raised her head, and then, with an enormous effort, she partially lifted her chest to face the boors, and instead of crying out in anger, she called out to God to help her.

She flailed her arms in a circular backward motion, losing her balance, and she toppled over onto the riverbank. The boys froze, waiting to see what would happen next. Carina managed to roll over, and they watched with trepidation as she was able to get on her feet again. Their fun had dissipated, and a few of them even felt mindful of the possible tragic consequences of their wanton brutality. No longer enjoying themselves, they tore off from the scene of their wickedness, abandoning the stolen goods they had brought with them.

Carina wept and talked to the Lord as she gathered up her strewn flowers, and gazed ruefully on the beautiful, wasted bread and pastries bobbing down the Arno. Astonishingly, the nature of Carina's sob-syncopated monologue was to thank God for protecting her, rather than wailing and bemoaning her loss. Speaking out loud the scripture, "The Lord is my helper, so I will have no fear. What can mere people do to me?" buoyed Carina and gave her strength in the midst of this disaster.

As she saved her flowers, she realized that many of the peaches that were cast at her were only slightly bruised.

Using her skirt like an apron, Carina gathered them up. When she dragged herself up to the top of the stairs, she saw the satchel that the boys had left was half full of peaches. So, she had traded treats from the bakery for peaches. Delighted to find a blessing amidst her setback, Carina put her mishap behind her and looked forward to an afternoon of celebration. With her newfound satchel of perfumed peaches, she made her way slowly back to Piazza San Marco where Lydia and Samuele were anxiously waiting for her.

"Carina! What happened? Oh, my love, we were starting to worry." Lydia raised Carina's head and looked tenderly into her eyes. Carina seemed shaken, and Lydia did not have the heart to chide her tardiness, so she wrapped Carina in her shawl and Samuele helped her into their horse-drawn cart to return home.

Even though Carina had been cruelly abused and some of the peaches bruised, she sang to herself in anticipation of the joy of uplifting the spirits of those she had invited to join her at the Studio for their Sunday lunch.

Chapter Eight

Donatella stamped her feet, cast aside the doll she had been playing with and glared at Anna. She shook her head vigorously, her curly red hair flying. "I want to go to the banquet room," she demanded for the umpteenth time.

And once again Anna gritted her teeth and said in as soothing a voice as possible, "Please compose yourself. You will have the opportunity to visit with all the guests later on."

Donatella was an only child, and in her loneliness she looked forward to family get-togethers of any sort. She lived as the center of her world, and due to her noble position, she had never been oriented toward creating caring friendships with others outside her class. She paced the bedroom, fleetingly turned her attention back to her dolls and the intricately carved wooden dollhouse — a replica of a castle with turreted towers — and then ran to the casement window and stood on her tiptoes to observe the musicians in the palazzo courtyard below. They were setting up their instruments in anticipation of the evening's festivities, when an elaborate display of fireworks would light up all of Florence.

"Let us fix your hair nicely," said Anna as she once again tried to settle Donatella.

Donatella spun around, and with an expression on her face that was both angelic and wicked she announced, "You can't stop me."

Before she had a chance to respond, Donatella raced past Anna, dodging her arms, and flung open her bedroom door and bolted down the passageway. She danced down the ornate staircase, past the gilded portraits of her ancestors, with Anna huffing behind her.

Donatella dashed along the wide hallway and out into the courtyard where she stumbled and fell on the inlaid stones and scraped her knee. But that didn't stop her, and she quickly picked herself up and raced ahead. Anna had almost caught up with her when Donatella flung open the doors to the banquet room. Indifferent to the formal celebration lunch in progress with the noble family and their guests, Donatella made a beeline for her parents and plummeted into her mother's lap next to her father, Duke Eduardo. Blinking back tears, she raised her skirt to reveal her knee, attempting to make her little scrape appear to be a momentous tragedy worthy of the greatest sympathy by one and all.

Anna was not far behind, cowering at the impetuousness of Donatella's actions, knowing she was accountable for the safety of little Donatella and the correctness of her manners. Of course, the unexpected intrusion of Donatella aroused Duchess Lucrezia's attention, and while at first glaring disapprovingly at Anna, she then extended a consoling invitation to her granddaughter to sit beside her at the banquet table. One of the servants-in-waiting promptly set a place for her beside her grandmother, and feeling like a guest of the highest honor, Donatella took her seat and waved to the assembled guests. Lucrezia pulled a handkerchief from her pocket and daubed Donatella's scraped knee with some cooling water, and it was easily forgotten.

This Sunday feast at the palazzo was an event of lavish display, fitting for the festival of San Giovanni Battista, the patron saint of Florence. Ornamental marzipan figures adorned with the family crest decorated the table with its gold and blue cloths. Servants attired in formal habit whisked in and out whilst refreshing the guests' wine glasses with the finest decanted wines. At the far end of the table, the Maestro conversed politely with other notable members of Florentine society while Pietro, quite enthralled by the proceedings, stood close by, ready to assist the Maestro should he have a need. The elaborate nature of the celebration was far more luxurious than anything Pietro had seen before in his family's gatherings, and he was elated to be present.

Fanfare accompanied the appearance of delectable dishes, and between courses a quartet of musicians entertained the diners, but the noble family and guests seemed to take it all for granted. Duke Onorio sat sadly beside Lucrezia, never having reacquired a lust for life after the death of his beloved Duchess Grazia. Regardless of the multitude of opportunities to remarry and develop a new, and perhaps even better life, he'd chosen to withdraw from enjoying his life. Seeing the Duke like this pained the Maestro. Like Onorio, the Maestro had chosen not to remarry after the death of his wife, but his artistic gifts gave him fulfillment and satisfaction. He did not grieve anymore, but rather rejoiced at the beauty that flowed through and around him at the Studio.

With her granddaughter now by her side, Lucrezia sat tall, while her roving eagle eye did not miss a single detail of activity. She criticized faults in the preparation and presentation of the dishes coming forth, interrupting her already fretful conversation to complain to her guests and to the servants about some unimportant this or some insignificant that. She could just as easily have praised the excellence and innovation of the more exotic dishes of eggs in aspic, semolina soufflé, gnocchi and ravioli of artichoke and ricotta, and heralded the artistic merits of the more carefully crafted display platters.

Rather than embellishing this feast with her wit and charm, young Duchess Donatella fidgeted restlessly, grouching that the meal was taking too long. She wanted to move on to the real fun, the music and dancing.

The Maestro, in contrast, partook of the delights before him in an enthusiastic manner that one would only expect of a man much younger than he. After the main courses he lifted his glass to toast the generosity of the noble family. In his usual magnanimous manner, he then turned his attention to the servants, thanking them for their attentive service, and he even acknowledged the dogs for their good behavior. "Quite unlike the rascally pair we have at the Studio," he said to his dinner partner, a high-ranking cardinal seated beside him.

Servants entered with elaborate platters of desserts just as the tolling of bells from the Duomo reminded the Maestro of the hour, and of one of his favorite events of the week — Carina's Sunday afternoon beggars' banquet. Even though it would not compare with the lavish banquet at the palazzo, the love and joy generated by Carina and her beloved guests made it an event the Maestro rarely missed. Duty and the need to respect the ruling Florentine family prevented him, however, from leaving, and he graciously accepted a plate of chocolate-covered Florentines, amaretti and biscotti da Prato followed by espresso coffee and a choice of digestive drinks. This being the fourth celebration he'd attended at the palazzo and knowing the abundance of the desserts being offered, the Maestro had come prepared to carry home a treat for Carina and her Sunday guests. He discreetly slipped some of the sweets off his plate into a napkin he had brought with him, which he then stuffed into one of his ample pockets.

Donatella, jumping up from her seat beside the Duchess, indicated she was ready to get on to the dancing and games.

"Compliments on your granddaughter's beauty," the Maestro said to Duchess Lucrezia, as Donatella tugged at her hand.

Pietro, still at attention behind the Maestro's chair, had been enjoying the vision of the young Donatella, and he remarked in a somewhat inappropriately loud voice, "The Duchess Donatella would make an exquisite subject for a portrait, don't you think, Maestro?"

Donatella heard Pietro's comment and flashed a penetrating glance towards him, the Maestro and then her grandmother. Pietro smiled in recognition of his suggestion, and even Donatella's parents smiled back at him. "An excellent idea!" said the Maestro.

With the guests now moving to the courtyard, the Maestro gave his formal thanks to Duchess Lucrezia, and he and Pietro exited the ducal palazzo. Samuele was waiting with the Maestro's horse and cart, ready to take him home. He also had Pietro's horse, the plan being that Pietro would return to his family's palazzo in Via della Vigna Nuova. But with his suggestion of the portrait of Duchess Donatella being of interest to the Maestro and the noble family, Pietro decided to accompany the Maestro in his cart until he reached the street leading to his family home. Samuele tethered his horse to the cart, and with the shadows lengthening in the narrow streets they set off.

Around them the joyful citizens of Florence hurried to position themselves on the bridges that arched over the Arno, the best places to view the evening fireworks. The Maestro, however, could not forget how joyless the noble family seemed, and spoke of this to Pietro. "We have just dined at the most lavish banquet table in all of Florence. But unless the fellowship at the table is also nourishing and compliments the abundance, there is no satisfaction." Pietro, who would have preferred to hear the Maestro's thoughts as to how to proceed to get a commission to paint Duchess Donatella's portrait, listened dutifully. He was just about to ask about the portrait when they arrived at the entrance to Vigna della Nuova. He mounted his horse and bid a respectful goodbye to the Maestro, adding that he would see him the next morning for work at the Studio.

Chapter Nine

By the time the Maestro and Samuele returned home to the Studio, Carina's Sunday banquet was still in full swing with all her friends participating. Carina had crowned Lydia's head with a lovely garland fashioned from the flowers she had gathered at the Arno. Sister Clara was present as usual and had said grace over the meal before they began, which was usually the Maestro's privilege. She frequently brought a delicacy from the convent to add to Carina's "banquet" fare. Today, in honor of the festa of San Giovanni, she had brought a Torta della Nonna, a simple but favorite Florentine dessert.

Hearing the horse cart arrive in the courtyard, Carina hurried to the front door to welcome the Maestro. She led him into the kitchen, proudly pointing out her flower-bedecked table. As he admired it she glanced nervously at Lydia, worried that Lydia would speak of her mishap with the hooligans by the banks of the Arno. But Lydia, who had intricately woven Carina's hair into fine French braids, looked at her with love and pride, and Carina knew the Sunday feast would proceed as normal. She showed the Maestro the bounty of peaches — some arranged in a bowl, the bruised ones stewed with fragrant spices. The Maestro then unveiled his surprise package of sweets taken from the banquet at the noble family's palazzo.

With the arrival of the Maestro, cries of delight filled the kitchen from the group of folks attending Carina's beggars' banquet. Grateful for his presence, the little tattered band welcomed him with kisses, curtsies and bows and made a place for him at the head of the table. The dwarf, Solomon, sat at his right. He'd been given a special chair piled with pillows so he could eat at the table comfortably. Next to him was limping Sara, whose one short leg had made her an object of ridicule for years. Sara worked for the town butcher, and she always did her best to add to the cauldron her offering of a few meat bones. Seated next to Sara was tall and skinny Stefano who'd lost an eye and, as a result, was often the butt of numerous jokes made by insensitive people. Deaf Rodolfo did his best to communicate with strange barking croaks, accompanied by elegant hand gestures which Carina could now interpret and understand. Amelia who was deaf from birth, Filippo with a shortened leg, and one-armed Samson came next. Sister Clara sat between blind Delmonico and old Maria, both of whom needed Sister Clara's assistance to feed themselves. Lydia and Carina remained on their feet, ready to meet the needs of their beloved guests. The warm quality of love that drew these folks together contrasted sharply with the cool atmosphere of the banquet that the Maestro had just attended at the royal palazzo. Each one present sought refuge here with Carina at the Maestro's Studio where they were welcomed wholeheartedly, without prejudice.

A knock on the back door briefly interrupted the joyful proceedings, as Adamo, who had managed to come from Florence, joined them all. Carina greeted him enthusiastically and made sure there was room for him at the table.

It was a crowded, cozy atmosphere and all preferred to eat in the kitchen, close together, rather than supping in the more stately-proportioned dining hall. The Maestro, quite satiated from the banquet at the palazzo, brought his drawing pad to the table, and while the others guzzled the lovingly stirred stew Carina had prepared, he deftly wielded his charcoal, already sketching out his idea of a musical instrument for Carina. Carina peeked at his sketch pad and exclaimed, "Maestro is going to make me a musical instrument. Oh, joy!"

When they were finished with the stew and the peaches and the sweets from the palazzo's banquet, everyone around the table stretched and patted their full bellies. Carina looked at the Maestro and Sister Clara and asked, "May I close the meal with a prayer of thanksgiving? Our being here all together gives me such delight, and I would like to give thanks unto the Lord." Carina prayed in her unique and personal way, thanking God for His unfailing care and for providing bountiful nourishment.

What would a banquet be without entertainment? After the table was cleared, the guests called out for Carina to sing. She might have appeared shy to those she met outside the Studio, but here Carina loved to entertain and bring joy. She had composed a new song and happily shared it with her friends.

> Even when I'm walking, even when I'm
>   talking, praise God, I'm praising God.
> Even when I'm singing, even when I'm
>   dancing, praise God, I'm praising God.
> And why don't you, praise God too? And
>   why don't you praise God too?
> Courage, my love, la la la la,
> Courage, mon cher, la la la la,
> Coraggio, mio caro, the Lord is there!

She inspired each one at the table to take a turn at kicking up their heels or their peg-leg or whatever! Even deaf Rodolfo took a whirl at balancing a peach on his nose, and what had once been a source of cruel amusement, now was transformed into an object of refreshing entertainment at Carina's party. It was a celebratory time, full of amusing antics and loving exchanges.

Exhausted, Carina called in Buono and Buona from outside, and plopped herself down by the fire to feed the dogs a few leftover morsels. She asked Lydia to help her position herself so she could lean back against the hearth stones, basking in the fire's heat. Carina's head rolled back against the wall, and she took a nap right in the middle of the lighthearted fun. This did not go unnoticed by the Maestro, and he studied Carina's face, sketching her as the glow from the fire bathed her fair, fine features in soft light.

After a pause in their afternoon fellowship and with the sun having set, the entire group moved outside to view the fireworks in the valley below. What an enthralling vision! The sky lit up with a continual flow of stunning, flamboyant colored flames accompanied by booming, blasting accompaniment.

Chapter Ten

Lucrezia awakened early before dawn the next day. The banquet had been a success, even though she'd had to harangue and scold the servants and make sure everything arrived on time. The Maestro and her other honored guests seemed pleased, but she felt weary, tired of leading her branch of familial nobility. Reassessing the previous day's festivities, she realized, once again, that it was a heavy responsibility for her as a woman, and she missed her husband. Her marriage had been arranged, as was the custom of the time, and had never blossomed into love. She'd made peace with that. But the two of them had moments of companionship that she thought of now with longing. Her husband had been dead for how many years? It shocked her that she could not remember. She resumed her critical reflection of the previous day's events. The Maestro had left so soon after the dessert course, and then one of the musicians had broken a string on his lute and she'd heard that false note and winced. Ah, but the fireworks! They had been magnificent, lighting up the night sky, visible for miles. This thought brought a momentary joy to her heart, but then she remembered her granddaughter's behavior. Anna, so loyal to her over the years, had been clearly struggling to control Donatella. But hadn't Lucrezia herself been an excitable young girl? Memories of her childhood under the control of her own governess flashed before her. Donatella was just like her!

A soft knock on the door told her Anna was about to enter. Lucrezia closed her eyes, at first pretending to be asleep. Anna always drew the heavily brocaded drapes open with force, the morning light flooding the room. She heard Anna set the breakfast tray on the table beside the window, but Lucrezia had no interest in eating. Instead, she opened her eyes, raised an eyebrow, and greeted Anna.

"Good morning, Duchess," Anna said, as she poured a cup of coffee for Lucrezia. "The whole town is still talking about last night's fireworks."

"Yes, yes." Lucrezia dismissed this good report with a wave of her hand. Still gazing at the ceiling, she spoke: "Even though she is only eleven," she paused for dramatic effect, "it is not too soon to be thinking about arranging a marriage for Donatella."

At these words Anna ceased her hustle and bustle about the room in preparation for Lucrezia's morning toilette. Lucrezia watched her intently. Anna was one of her closest confidantes, her loyalty secured through intense times of political struggle, and she valued Anna's opinions. "And who do you think would be the most suitable mate for her?"

"Forgive me, Duchess, but I could not possibly guess."

"The young Duke Massimo of Siena, of course!"

Anna was aware of all the noble families in Florence and Siena, but she had not met young Duke Massimo. "How old is he?"

"Anna, Anna, always so practical." Lucrezia smiled slyly. "He is several years older than Donatella. There was a suggestion yesterday by the Maestro's assistant to have a portrait of stunning little Donatella painted. Good idea! Perhaps I should ask the Maestro to do so, and we can present it to the young Duke and his family as a gift. Yes, I think it's time to start negotiations. In fact, I think there should be an exchange of portraits. Don't you, Anna?"

"Yes, of course. What a brilliant idea," Anna replied, even as she silently questioned her mistress's impetuousness.

"We will go today then. Go prepare Donatella to visit the Maestro's Studio, and dress her in her most magnificent beaded collar. We will leave after breakfast."

Within the morning hour Lucrezia, Donatella, and Anna, accompanied by palazzo guards, made their way in their carriage through the streets of Florence up to the Maestro's Studio in Settignano. Lucrezia did not invite Donatella's mother, Duchess Francesca, to join them, as she was pregnant with her second child and needed bed rest. Donatella at first was not fully aware of the purpose of their visit, but it was a glorious day full of sunshine, and this was a welcome outing. She relished the waves from those they passed but soon grew fidgety, until Lucrezia explained to Donatella her intention to have the Maestro paint a portrait of her.

"Of me?" Donatella exclaimed. "Wonderful! How exciting! Am I dressed properly?"

They wended their way through the countryside toward Settignano, passing fields of lavender that perfumed the air. At the top of the hill a huge fig tree, fully leafed out and budding with figs, framed the view of the piazza of Settignano. They proceeded through the piazza to arrive at the Maestro's home on the far edge of the town.

The Maestro's Studio was in full activity and the Maestro had already selected and begun shaping the wood for the instrument that was to become Carina's dulcimer. His protégés were present, busy working on their sketches and exercising various aspects of the craft of painting as they studied the still life with props he'd set up for them.

As was now her custom, Carina passed through the Studio with a small bowl asking for alms for the next Sunday's beggars' banquet. She approached each one of the students, tugging at their smocks, reminding them to share with those less fortunate than they. The Maestro paused his work on her instrument and set the example by pulling a coin from his pocket and plunking it down in her little bowl. The other artists followed suit, some responding more generously than others. Only Pietro ignored her, because he still considered her Sunday gathering to be a blight on the Studio's reputation. This was the only time Carina plucked up the courage to directly interact with the Studio activities, and with her request of alms completed, she returned to her household chores in the kitchen. This morning she needed to clean the water closet, which was quite a challenge for Carina, but she tended to her assigned household duties with responsibility and without lament. She managed, with difficulty, to fill the water buckets and got busy making sure all the floor tiles were clean.

Lydia was in the kitchen when the barking of Buono and Buona drew her attention. Through the window she saw an ornate carriage drawn by two fine horses approaching the Maestro's home. It came to halt, and she recognized the young duchess and her grandmother, and she hurried outside to stop the dogs from jumping up with their muddy paws. She led Lucrezia and her entourage into the Studio and then retreated to a corner. Pietro quickly mustered order in the ranks of the excited students and then stood stalwart beside the Maestro in his painter's chair as they greeted Lucrezia, Donatella and Anna.

Lucrezia, without being invited to do so, prompted little Donatella to stand on the model's platform. "Dear Maestro, you will remember that yesterday at our luncheon banquet your assistant suggested a portrait of Duchess Donatella be painted. I think this is an excellent idea." She explained to the Maestro, taking for granted that he would not refuse, that her intention was to present it to the ducal family of Siena. "I am also commissioning you to paint a portrait of young Duke Massimo, the impending heir to the house of Siena."

How could the Maestro object? A royal commission was always welcome. He explained, however, that he was too old in years to foray to Siena to paint Massimo's portrait. "Would it be possible for the young duke to come pose for me here in Florence?" he asked.

"I have anticipated your need," Lucrezia declared. She intended that very day to send a sealed scroll to the Grand Duke of Siena, requesting his presence in Florence, along with his wife and his son, Massimo.

Donatella loved being the center of attention on the posing platform, and she arranged her skirts so as to continue to attract the enchanted gazes of the young painters. Pietro rigidly drew himself up. He was very interested in this portrait exchange, hoping that these young nobles would someday be future commissioners of his artwork and portraiture. He offered to make the ride to Siena to present Lucrezia's request to the ducal family, but Lucrezia scoffed at his impertinence and excused herself to return to the palazzo to complete the initiation of her plans, leaving Anna to attend Donatella as she began sitting for her portrait sketches. As Lucrezia left, arrangements were made for her guards to return with their carriage to eventually bring Anna and Donatella home to the palazzo. Assuming that this was no imposition upon the Studio's schedule, Lucrezia did not even consider that this might not be a good time for the Maestro to commence working on Donatella's portrait.

And so the preliminary sketches for the portrait began. Posing, for young Donatella, was not easy. A half hour into the session she was bored, twisting and turning and sighing, and Anna had to constantly coax her to be still. The Maestro handled Donatella's discomfort with the gracious aplomb and sensitivity characteristic of him, choosing to ignore Donatella's less attractive antics, and thereby gaining her confidence.

Lydia was not at all thrilled to have this female intrusion in her domain. But she recognized that any new commission for a painting was good for the financial stability of the Studio, so she did her best to facilitate Donatella and Anna's presence.

At last, sitting became too much for Donatella, and she whispered a request that Anna arrange for her to be excused to go use the water closet. Not knowing where it was, Anna demanded that Lydia lead the way for Donatella, who minced out of the Studio, following Lydia.

Entering the back corridor, Lydia indicated the water closet at the end of the hall and then waited for the young duchess. Donatella pulled the door open, surprising Carina who was still inside, hunched over and cleaning. Both young girls reeled back, Carina knocking over her pails and brooms and Donatella shrieking for Anna. She fled from this strange crippled being and ran past Lydia to return to the Studio and Anna's arms.

The Maestro and Lydia tried to apologize, but Donatella's cries as she wailed about the frightful girl she had seen in the water closet drowned out all reason. Anna brought the portrait session to an immediate close, and the Maestro offered his horse and cart to accompany them back to their palazzo in Florence.

The idea of the young duchess riding back to the palazzo in the Maestro's humble cart incensed Pietro. Surely this was the way commissions were lost. Ignoring the Maestro's request that he calm himself, he stormed into the kitchen and found Carina. "How dare you upset the Duchess Donatella?"

Carina shrank back. "What did I do? I was just cleaning here when —"

"It's a good thing you had already partaken of your habit of begging before the Duchess Lucrezia arrived," Pietro fumed. "We wouldn't want the ducal household to know we had such goings on here."

Deeply wounded by his words, Carina dropped the rag she had been clutching, and weeping, she quickly made her way to the room that she shared with Lydia. In the Studio, the Maestro urged his students to get back to their sketches while Pietro hurried out onto the road and watched the cart and the young fiery-haired duchess receding from view, along with, to his mind, his possibility of ever getting a commission from the ducal family.

In the quiet and dark of the bedroom, Carina threw herself on her sleeping pallet at the foot of Lydia's bed. She buried her head between her knees, covered her head with a pillow, and sobbed. Pietro's cruelty to her felt devastating.

What did he know about being wanted? What did he know about hard work? He didn't have to beg. He knew nothing about her suffering or how hard her life was, how every day was a challenge. Closing her eyes and covering her heart with her hands, she breathed deeply before speaking out loud. "Lord God, I have no desire to hate Pietro. Help me to love him. I forgive him, Lord. I forgive him. He doesn't mean to hurt me. He just doesn't know any better."

Rolling to her feet, she straightened her bedding and made her way out to the garden, Carina's place of consolation. She collected a bouquet of fragrant flowers to adorn the kitchen table as a gesture of love for Lydia and the Maestro.

Unaware of Carina's tears, Lydia reentered the kitchen to prepare lunch. She couldn't shake her annoyance, and she chopped vegetables with quiet fury as she prepared the sauce for the day's pasta. She always wanted to keep calm and order in the house, and the intrusion of the Duchess and her entourage had upset her plan for the day. She knew the Maestro needed these commissions and the money helped keep the Studio running smoothly, but the lack of good manners and their impudence rankled her.

Through the window she saw Pietro stomping up the path outside. Another one with no consideration!

"It's your fault! They left without saying goodbye to me!" Pietro said as he barged into the kitchen.

She reached for another knife and chopped with more vigor. "Why should they care? Who are you to them?"

He shook his head and marched back to the Studio.

With a pounding heart, Lydia managed to take a deep breath and carefully put her knife down on the table. Her anger had flared, but she caught her words and instead rushed off to her bedroom. She closed the door behind her, and now it was her turn to sprawl on the bed and weep. The door opened quietly after a few minutes, and Lydia sat up and saw Carina hunched over and holding forth a bouquet of wildflowers. Seeing her beloved Lydia so distraught alarmed Carina, but she did not budge, and quickly her worry transformed into loving concern for her dear friend. Carina set her bouquet on the night table and gave Lydia a tender kiss on her cheek.

"It is so hard when people are mean and don't care that I have feelings too," Lydia lamented.

With a gentle smile Carina said, "I understand. But there is someone much more loving and caring than me to help you."

"Who?"

"God. He cares for us with loving kindness. We can trust Him. We can talk to Him about all our deep and hurting things, and He answers our prayers." Carina looked steadfastly at Lydia and reached out and touched Lydia's tear-stained face. Then she took Lydia's hand and prayed. "Lord, God. We thank you for your love and your many blessings and mercies. We thank you that you are here with us, to strengthen, encourage and comfort us. We ask, Lord God, that we would be more sensitive to believe, so that we would know that we have a friend to help us, always with us. And, Lord, I ask you to heal Lydia of all the hurts inside her that are too deep for anybody to touch but you, Lord. And, please, God, help us to be loving, even to those who are hard to love."

Carina's words were a healing balm for Lydia, and her anger and pain melted. "What you say and pray is true, dear heart. Thank you."

They hugged one another, and Carina brought her bouquet of flowers closer to Lydia so she could smell their fragrance.

Chapter Eleven

Towards the end of the summer, arrangements were made for the Sienese ducal family to come to Florence. Due to the historic antagonism between Siena and Florence, eighteen-year-old Massimo had not previously visited Florence, but now there was a period of peace between the two cities. He gazed out of the carriage windows as he and his parents, the Duke and Duchess of Siena, journeyed through the glorious Tuscan countryside with its tall, elegant cypress trees. When the city of Florence came into view, with the towering Duomo and the Arno River and its beautiful bridges, he declared, "How beautiful the city of Florence is!" He'd been told the intention of their visit: a meeting with the Florentine ducal family to discuss matters of the State of Tuscany, with plans hopefully to reach an arrangement for his marriage to the Duchess Donatella. Reaching out to lay her hand upon her son's knee, his mother spoke to him softly. "Surely you will enjoy meeting the Duchess Lucrezia and her granddaughter, Duchess Donatella, and her sons, the Dukes Onorio and Eduardo." The Duke and Duchess of Siena were proud of their eldest son, Massimo, as not only was he handsome and proficiently athletic, but his character was distinguished by kindness and consideration for others, rare qualities for someone still coming into his manhood.

As the Sienese carriage entered through the main gate and pulled to a clamorous stop in the courtyard, the palazzo guards signaled their arrival with welcoming shouts of greeting. Hearing the noise from the stir of activity below, Duchess Lucrezia and Dukes Onorio and Eduardo descended and exited into the courtyard to welcome them. Both families then made their way to one of the receiving rooms to have refreshments and exchange greetings.

Portraits of the noble family lined the hallways in heavy gilded frames, and Massimo stopped to look at several of them, appreciating their beautiful artistry. When they reached the reception room, he spun around slowly to admire the frescoes on the vaulted ceiling. He turned to his father, his eyes aglow, and whispered to him, "Magnificent!"

After sipping refreshments and exchanging greetings, the Duke and Duchess of Siena retired to their guest quarters for an afternoon rest. Young Massimo declined this offer. Instead, he wandered through the ceremonial rooms of the ground floor to admire the décor and the artwork. Although Siena had their own acclaimed artists, this was his first experience of the extraordinary talents of Florentine artists.

With the tolling of the bells from the Duomo announcing the evening's hour, the two families gathered in the main banquet room for dinner. There was warm cordiality between the two families, and Donatella, attended by Anna, also made her well-orchestrated entrance for dinner, almost skipping with enthusiasm. At the end of the meal, the Duke and Duchess of Siena presented an offering of gifts to the noble ladies of the Florentine family, including an intricately tooled necklace for Donatella who showed her gratitude by performing delicate little curtsies.

Duchess Lucrezia and the Duke and Duchess of Siena retired alone after dinner to begin discussion of the proposed future betrothal of Massimo and Donatella. At first, there was a moment of tension, considering that Siena had recently been conceded to Florence by Spain, but the known intention of this meeting was to improve Florentine-Sienese diplomatic relations. When Lucrezia announced her desire for a family exchange of portraits of Massimo and Donatella to be painted by the celebrated Maestro of Settignano, the atmosphere relaxed, as both the Duke and Duchess of Siena knew of the Maestro's skill and reputation. Pleased that her plan was accepted, Lucrezia sent a messenger to the Maestro's Studio requesting that he send someone the very next day to escort the Sienese ducal family to the Studio so he could begin work on young Duke Massimo's portrait.

When Pietro arrived the following morning, he found Massimo in the courtyard where the guards were demonstrating to him how to throw into the air and catch the unfurled banners that were part of the fanfare accompanying the annual Calcio e Costume Storico, a rough and tumble ball game played by the Florentine aristocrats. At first Pietro watched from a distance. The young Duke seemed a rather pallid fellow in his assessment. Soon Pietro could not resist displaying his skills, and he barged in and grabbed a banner from a palazzo guard. The banner unfurled as he tossed it high and then caught it adroitly. Seeing he was fairly expert, the palazzo guards tossed their banners back and forth with Pietro, creating quite a show for Massimo who had moved to the sidelines to watch with his parents and young Donatella. They were interrupted as the ducal carriage arrived to escort Massimo and his parents up to the Maestro's Studio.

With a bow to Donatella, Pietro mounted his horse. Always appreciative of attention, she laughed and tossed her head, her curls catching the sunlight — that is, until she realized the guests were leaving without her and she stomped her foot, complaining bitterly as Anna tried to usher her back into the palazzo.

Hoping to continue his favor with the Florentine noble family, Pietro assured her, "We already have the preliminary sketches for your portrait, and it will be stunning."

The palazzo guards helped Massimo and his parents enter their carriage. With a gallant wave to Donatella, Pietro led the way to Settignano and the Maestro's Studio.

Chapter Twelve

Up in Settignano the final preparations were underway for the visit from the Sienese family. To create a feeling of tranquility and spaciousness for the sitting of Massimo's portrait, several of the students had left and only a few of the younger artists were helping Lydia and Carina put the Studio in order. Easels and studies in progress, however, remained on display, for if all were to go well with the Maestro's sketches, the work would continue in the Studio as usual the next day. The Maestro sat oblivious to the activity around him as he continued to work on his current painting of "The Madonna with Child and Angel." Carina's face and her crown of curls were easily recognizable as the inspiration for the painting's angel.

When the ducal family arrived along with Pietro, the Maestro welcomed them graciously. The Maestro seated the Grand Duke and Duchess in a comfortable position to observe, and he helped Massimo to get seated and posed for the initial sketches. Massimo was wide-eyed as he gazed about the Studio, it being his first time in such a creative environment. He particularly admired the Maestro's painting in progress and the sensitive portrayal of the Madonna. Lydia served wine and fruits and sweet dainties, while Carina remained in the kitchen, too shy to enter.

Over the years the Maestro developed certain ploys to keep his subjects from tiring and losing enthusiasm for the difficult discipline of posing, music being one of them. The Maestro had followed through on his promise and shaped a 4-stringed dulcimer for Carina. It was easy to tune, and she could lay the instrument on her lap. He designed a chair specially to accommodate her shape so she could play the instrument comfortably. Oh, what joy when the day arrived, and he presented it to her. "Thank you, thank you, dear Maestro! This is the sweetest sound I have ever heard," she exclaimed as she strummed it. Carina was soon composing songs full of fun and praise.

He now instructed Lydia to ask Carina if she would play her dulcimer so as to entertain them. How could one not oblige the Maestro? But Carina remembered the last time a ducal family had visited, and the way Duchess Donatella had shrieked when Carina startled her. She couldn't bear another response like that, so Lydia had the task of convincing an extremely reluctant Carina to come in and accompany them. It was not an easy job. But after a tear or two and the whispered expression of a few fears, after saying a prayer and letting go of uncomfortable cares, Carina picked up her dulcimer. With her head hanging low she followed Lydia into the Studio, where Lydia then placed the specially designed chair near the posing platform.

Not having been trained in music, Carina was a primitive who only knew how to pour out her heart. She gently strummed her sweet dulcimer's strings and sang softly. The Maestro had placed Carina in Massimo's line of sight so that he would continue to focus in the direction that was the best angle for the Maestro's sketches. Everyone was touched by her original melodies and uniquely personal lyrics. The music touched Carina's heart as well. Filled with gratitude, she overcame her shyness and stole a look at Massimo. He smiled back at her. She would have loved to befriend him if she could, but she dared not. Massimo seemed to accept her comfortably. He commented that the Maestro had made good use of his servant when he recognized Carina's face as the model for the angel in the Maestro's current painting.

Carina had also managed to bring her alms bowl in one of her smock's pockets. When the Maestro nodded at Carina, indicating she should take a rest, she put the dulcimer aside and outstretched her alms bowl to the Maestro, almost toppling over when she tried to curtsy before him. Pietro cringed, but Carina broke the tension of the moment, addressing the Maestro, "Please be so kind as to contribute an offering for those less fortunate than you."

Being a whole-hearted supporter, the Maestro dug his hand into his pocket and then dropped several coins in her bowl. Speaking to the ducal family, the Maestro explained, "Our dear Carina, who I have adopted as my daughter, is asking for help for her midday meal here at the Studio. Every Sunday she invites her needy and handicapped friends to come and enjoy fellowship and fun. I call her 'Our Lady of the Outcasts.'"

Pietro's face started to turn red out of embarrassment, but he felt obliged to follow the example, and he begrudgingly dropped a coin into Carina's offering bowl. Carina took courage and approached the Sienese Duke with her alms bowl, but the Duke's pockets were empty, as he had no money with him. The Sienese Duchess was quick to act, and without hesitation and in full view of all in the Studio, she took off from her hand one of her wondrously bejeweled rings and dropped it into Carina's outstretched bowl. Carina heard the Duchess's ring plunk into her bowl but did not realize the enormity of this generous donation. Carina then gingerly, but with a determination that was especially her own, approached Massimo. At first, he made a gesture as if to say he had nothing for her, but then, following his mother's example, he slipped off his gold signet ring and dropped it into Carina's bowl. Again, Carina heard something dropping into the bowl, and she twisted her head around to look up and thank him. She then retreated through the kitchen to the bedroom to examine her offerings.

The Maestro, however, saw with clarity that the Duchess and Massimo had deposited their valuable rings in Carina's alms bowl. Before he could object, the Duke spoke on behalf of his family: "Please accept our donations as given freely and in the spirit of generosity. Consider them, Maestro, our contribution to the portrait you will be painting of our son, Massimo."

Surprised by this turn of events, the Maestro made an on-the-spot decision to avoid embarrassment and agree to the ducal family's beneficent gestures. "Thank you ever so much for your kind generosity. You cannot imagine how you have blessed Carina by supporting her charitable Sunday lunch. I will oversee the use of the rings you have donated."

In the privacy of the bedroom and well away from the Studio, Carina tumbled the bowl's contents onto Lydia's bed, bringing a candle close for examination. Wonderstruck, she saw the lustrous gleam of rubies and sapphires reflected in the candlelight as she picked up the first ring. By the size of it, she could tell that it had been given by the Duchess.

Then she caught the gleam of the gold Sienese signet ring. Carina knew the source was Massimo. Carina clutched it to her heart, got up on her feet, and still bent over as ever, she did a little waltzing dance, holding her hand in front of her face as if she were dancing with a partner.

Lydia burst in the door, full of questions. She needed Carina's help to get the fire in the kitchen stoked up. She also wanted a closer look at the rings, as she too had been astonished by the ducal family's generosity, and she joined Carina on the bed.

"Think of it!" exclaimed Carina. "Now we can invite ALL the orphans and lots of old people to the Sunday banquet!"

Lydia alternated between delighting in the rings and fretting over whether they could keep them. She had heard the conversation between the Maestro and the duke, but she intended to receive the Maestro's permission concerning this matter. Lydia took the Duchess's bejeweled ring from Carina who loathed to part with it, but trusting her, she let loose of it. Lydia gazed intently at the ring. She looked at Carina, and then, at the ring again. Carina knew Lydia well enough to guess that some idea was hatching in her mind. Carina begged to coddle the ring once again. Lydia complied, and Carina held the ring up to the candlelight, basking in the glowing rubies and sapphires. Then once again she held Massimo's gold ring up to the candle, which shed more light on it.

As she stroked the ring with a tender touch, Lydia knew that Carina also longed to be tenderly stroked. Lydia's heart ached. The idea of her beloved Carina living her life severely handicapped, and thus isolated and vulnerable, grieved Lydia. By God's grace, surely there must be a way to help her.

Back in the Studio, the time had come for the initial portrait sketches of Massimo to conclude. "The light is changing," the Maestro declared, "and the young duke has been admirable in sitting for so long!" While Pietro prepared to accompany them back to Florence, the Maestro bid the Duke and Duchess and Massimo farewell. "I humbly thank you for your presence here today, and especially for your magnanimous generosity towards Carina and her needy friends."

"It is our privilege," responded the Duke.

Lydia and Carina were still sitting on Lydia's bed admiring the rings when the Maestro knocked gently at the bedroom door.

"Look, Maestro!" Carina exclaimed. Extending her hand to the Maestro, "See the magnificent ring the Duchess has donated."

"Yes, Carina," he answered tenderly.

Lydia interrupted, "But Maestro, can we really keep the ring? And there is another gold one given by the young Duke Massimo."

"Yes, Lydia, the ducal family insist that they be able to exercise generosity and give the rings freely."

"Now we can transform our Sunday meal celebration into a real banquet," exclaimed Carina. "And I have another idea! We can buy shoes and some new clothes for Rodolfo and Sara."

"Sweet, sweet Carina," Lydia said, and she took Carina's little hand in hers. "I too have an idea. The sale of these rings will surely bring in a significant amount of money." She paused, eyes on the Maestro who looked at her with curiosity and nodded for her to continue. She then glanced at Carina and saw how she sat there wide-eyed. The Sunday celebration was Carina's creative and emotional outlet, and she was frightened that her dream was being jeopardized.

Lydia chose her words carefully. "Beloved Carina, the Maestro and I love you dearly and have been amazed from the day you arrived that you managed to survive and sustain life, considering the physical condition that has been dealt you. But, dear heart, who is to say that you cannot surpass all expectations and walk upright? Yes, we can set aside a portion of this money for your Sunday events, but I propose we take the bulk of it to Doctor Benedetto. He is retired now and has not seen you in years. He is a gifted doctor and he surely has your well-being at heart.

Carina was stunned. All her life she had assumed that she must tolerate her torturous physical condition, and no serious attempt had been made until now to provide her with help to escape her disabilities. Certainly surprise, hope, excitement, and the possible realization of a secret desire welled up within Carina, mixed with fear.

The Maestro had been listening intently and now intervened. "You came into my life unexpectedly, and you are precious to us. Lydia is right. This is an opportunity for a transformation in your life, both physically and emotionally. I will go into Florence to sell the Duchess's ring tomorrow."

A moment of silence fell upon them. The Maestro, Lydia and Carina all closed their eyes and bent their heads pensively in prayer.

The Maestro spoke, "Thank you, Lord. Lead and guide us, and may the finances from this ring be used according to your purposes and be a blessing to Carina."

They agreed with an 'amen,' and Carina reached out her hand and relinquished the ring to the Maestro.

There was no discussion about Massimo's ring, but a particular inspiration had come into the Maestro's mind regarding Massimo's portrait. Because of his extraordinary generosity, the Maestro intended to include Massimo's ring on his hand in his portrait, highlighted by the use of gold leaf.

The next morning the Maestro left the Studio and his students to be overseen by Pietro, while he and Samuele rode his cart into Florence to go to the Ponte Vecchio where the Maestro knew a jeweler, from whom he had bought gold leaf when he needed it for his fresco work in his parish church and private chapel commissions. Because the Maestro was well known by the jeweler, there was no uncertainty about the validity of the Maestro's ownership of the ring. The Maestro bought some gold leaf as part of the cash sale, and he shared with the jeweler his plan to use it in the portrait for the Sienese ducal family.

Upon returning to the Studio with Samuele, the Maestro immediately sought out Lydia and Carina. "The ring sale went well," he shared. "Lydia, I will write a letter for Doctor Benedetto, and I would like for you to go with Samuele up to his home and ask him to come and meet with Carina here."

The decision had been made, and Carina could not object.

Chapter Thirteen

The following day Lydia and Samuele made the journey up to the remote hills of Fiesole outside Florence. Although they were on an errand for the Maestro, the day took on the feeling of an outing of two friends. Samuele had been working for the Maestro for ten years before Lydia arrived. He had come to know the Maestro through their church parish in Settignano, as he helped many in the community with their horse and stable needs. He and his wife had four children, so he was fatherly in nature and fond of both Lydia and Carina. With Lydia sitting on one of the bench seats in the cart, Samuele whistled as he guided Golden Slippers up the increasingly steep hill, urging him to hold steady. When the track leveled out, he settled into an easy pace.

Samuele sensed that Lydia was preoccupied, heavy laden with thought. He invited her to sit beside him on the cart bench so she could have conversation with him if she needed it. It would take at least another hour to make the trip to Doctor Benedetto's home where, in retirement, he continued his research and tended to his vineyard and orchard.

As Lydia clutched the Maestro's letter intended for the doctor, she explained to Samuele the purpose of the day's mission. "I worry though. What if there is nothing Doctor Benedetto can do for her? Who will take care of Carina when the Maestro and I are gone? How will she survive?"

Samuele sighed deeply. "This world is so challenging. My wife and I have enjoyed our children ever so much, and yet we too have moments of anguish over their well-being and concern for their futures. It's the nature of being a parent."

"Carina is like a daughter to me and the Maestro," Lydia responded, briefly closing her eyes, and covering her heart with her hand. "She is the daughter I never had."

The doctor's villa was easily found at the end of a long road nestled amongst his vineyards. Samuele helped Lydia dismount as he waited outside. Lydia knocked on the door, and the doctor's wife answered and invited her in. Contraptions from Doctor Benedetto's research and numerous body braces in various stages of development crowded the reception area. Doctor Benedetto immediately recognized Lydia and came to greet her.

"How is the Maestro doing?" he asked.

"Aging, but well, thank you," Lydia replied. "He asked me to deliver this letter to you. It concerns Carina."

Doctor Benedetto indicated for Lydia to follow him into a side office where they seated themselves. He read the letter and nodded thoughtfully. "Of course I will evaluate her condition. Tell me Lydia, how many years has it been since I examined her?"

"I think it is about four years, Doctor Benedetto. She is very bent over and it is a big struggle for her, but she is full of life and has developed well mentally."

"And it is far too long since I have seen the Maestro. Tell him I will make the trip tomorrow."

Lydia thanked him, and she and Samuele made their way back down the winding road with several containers of olive oil freshly pressed from the doctor's groves.

The following day Carina was in her garden, gathering some herbs and lettuces for the day's lunch and tending to one of her cherished roses, when the sound of horse's hooves on the path alongside the garden wall drew her attention. She heard someone whistling and speaking to the horse. "There you go, girl. Here we are. I'll get you some water." Carina did not recognize this man's voice. Curious, she moved to the wall and hoisted herself up to take a look. She was surprised to find an elderly man staring back at her. Startled, she tumbled back, upsetting her basket of freshly picked greens.

"Good heavens, I am sorry!" he cried out. "I did not mean to startle you." With great agility, he climbed over the wall to help Carina.

She flinched, expecting him to recoil as strangers often did when they realized her physical handicap. Instead, the stranger helped her into a more comfortable position. And unlike so many others, he got down to her height. He knelt on the dirt in her garden and again asked if she was all right.

"Yes, yes," she assured him. She looked around hoping to see Lydia or the Maestro or even Pietro. She was still a little apprehensive about the stranger, but when she glanced up at his face again, she vaguely recognized him. "Doctor Benedetto?"

"Yes. it has been a while since I've seen you." Noting the orderliness and bounty of Carina's garden, Doctor Benedetto asked, "Is it you who tends this beautiful garden?"

When Carina answered, "Yes," he commented on the herb plot. "I see you have lots of medicinal herbs growing too."

"Medicinal herbs?" Carina asked.

"Yes, thyme, rosemary, sage. They all benefit healing and good health." "Oh, I didn't know. I always called this area 'Lydia's plot,' because she uses everything for her cooking. Now I will call it 'Lydia's Healing Garden.' I especially like the sage plants because they have beautiful purple flowers."

The voice of Lydia calling her name interrupted them.

"I am here!" responded Carina.

Lydia appeared and enthusiastically greeted the doctor. "Ah, Carina, is it possible that you would remember Doctor Benedetto? The Maestro and I have invited him to come and determine if there can be a way to heal you of your infirmities."

"Heal me?" Carina twisted her head to look intensely at the doctor, her questioning eyes opening wide with hope. "But first his horse is waiting for a good drink of water on the other side of the wall!"

Doctor Benedetto added, "Yes, and one of the saddle bags has a basket of fruits and vegetables from my garden for you!"

As Samuele led Doctor Benedetto's horse to the stables, the three of them made their way through the garden to the Studio where the Maestro eagerly waited to renew his friendship with the doctor. After a warm greeting they were soon chatting away about the recent discoveries in the fields of anatomy and engineering. On and on they talked, both being cultured scientific researchers. In the years since they had seen each other, the Maestro had developed a technique for hydrodynamics which he had put into use getting water from the garden well into the kitchen, and Doctor Benedetto had been busy with physical therapy analyses. And then they had to look at the produce the doctor had brought for them, including a new variety of plums, the sweetest of Doctor Benedetto's orchard.

"Try one!" the doctor insisted, and there was the Maestro with juice running down his chin, eyes closed in happiness as he bit into a deep purple prune.

Carina giggled. To see the Maestro in this moment of bliss pleased her. She looked at Lydia who shook her head and mouthed, "I wish they would hurry up," but she too was smiling.

Eventually Lydia cleared her throat and pushed Carina forward and both men exclaimed, "Ah, yes, Carina!"

With gentleness the Maestro asked Carina, "Would you be willing to let Doctor Benedetto examine you?"

Carina paused before responding to this unexpected visit and invitation, and then carefully nodded her head in agreement, her eyes fixed on Doctor Benedetto. At Lydia's suggestion, she and Carina and Doctor Benedetto retired to her bedroom for his medical evaluation.

He spoke gently to Carina, questioning her about her abilities when it came to doing the chores around the house. He asked about her bouts with pain; was there any activity in particular that brought it on? He measured her so as to better understand her deformed condition. When finished, Lydia and Carina watched anxiously as he contemplated his diagnosis.

Returning into the Studio to meet alone at first with the Maestro, the doctor asked him if it would be possible for them to collaborate on constructing an apparatus he had in mind for Carina. "I believe she is at the right age and is strong enough for us to proceed with a therapy program designed specifically for her." The doctor explained that

Carina's problem came from an extremely weak musculature, particularly throughout her upper back and along her spine. "Even though the weak musculature has caused her to constantly crouch over, Carina is not a classic hunchback with a locked spine. Because she has been working daily at heavy household chores, Carina's arms and legs have become very strong." Although she was thin, and her back accustomed to its "C" shape, Doctor Benedetto's analysis indicated Carina could have normal proportions if she could develop the strength to stand up straight.

The doctor then invited Carina to join them. He reiterated what he had told the Maestro and explained to Carina that if she diligently followed the therapeutic regime, she could strengthen her back, and, in accordance with her perseverance, she could reach a more normal stature. "You will need a brace which must be worn daily, although taken off when you sleep at night, and be readjusted every six months. You need to know that this procedure could cause some pain, and you will need to persevere with determination."

Would the Maestro work with him to invent an adjustable brace, asked Doctor Benedetto? The Maestro complied. Would Carina cooperate? All eyes focused on Carina. Her head hung low. Not answering, she requested that she be excused to think about it before answering.

Carina retired to her room where she sat on her bed. She spoke out, "Dear Lord, what am I to do? Is there hope for me?" She waited silently, her eyes closed, until she sensed a peace within. Carina took a deep breath, looked up and prayed, "Lord, I will work hard, if you will give me the ability to endure the pain. Thank you for Doctor Benedetto, Lydia, and the Maestro. Please lead and guide them as they help me and remind me always to be grateful for their loving care."

Carina slowly came back to the Maestro's study, a new confidence and determined step replacing her shuffle, to find the doctor and the Maestro already excitedly designing the apparatus. The flurry of conversation and the sound of charcoal scratching on paper ceased when Carina reentered the room.

"Well?" Lydia ventured.

Quietly, Carina replied, "I'm ready."

The doctor worked into the afternoon, taking several measurements. He sketched and conferred with the Maestro and then measured some more. He then asked Carina to perform her chores so he could observe her movement. He took copious notes and whenever she caught his eye he smiled and assured her. He left with a bouquet of her medicinal herbs that she picked especially for him. Both she and Lydia stood in the garden and watched until he and his horse were barely visible as they made their way along the ridge pathway back up to his home.

Several days later Doctor Benedetto returned with a chair designed especially for Carina. The Maestro helped him set it up in a well-lit corner of the Studio in front of Carina's embroidery loom. Sister Clara had suggested that Carina do embroidery as a possible therapeutic way to strengthen her back, but because of Carina being so bent over, she had not been able to work well at the embroidery loom. She'd felt so excited for this outlet of her creativity and had been disappointed at not being able to utilize the colored threads as a way of painting, as did the Maestro and all the others in the Studio. Now, due to the angle at which her embroidery stand was placed in relation to the height of the new chair, this love of hers to create beauty seemed a distinct possibility.

The Maestro, meanwhile, had been fashioning a device — as per the doctor's instructions — that would be Carina's back brace. It was cumbersome with its straps and buckles, but the brace could be adjusted at different angles, forcing Carina to hold herself more upright with each adjustment. She was daunted by it, but the doctor and the Maestro reassured her that she would get used to it and would be victorious in the end.

Chapter Fourteen

*A*utumn brought rainy weather and grey skies. The leaves in the Tuscan countryside turned scarlet and orange. This had often been a challenging time of year for Carina, the dampness creeping into her bones, causing her pain. But this year it was a joyful time, a time of possibility. With the Maestro's help she created a tapestry design of an abundance of autumn fruits of varied colors and hues, overflowing from a brightly designed bowl on a table. Even in those first days Carina noticed an improvement with her stature; the back brace and the chair helped lift up her body position when she sat at the embroidery loom. After hours at the loom her weakened back muscles ached, but she did not complain. Lydia massaged Carina in the evenings before bedtime when she took off her brace after a long day, hoping to alleviate the pain so Carina could sleep well.

With the support of the brace, Carina became more upright and stood taller month by month. Now when she stood at the far end of the kitchen, Carina felt much encouraged because she could see the sunset of the gold and pink-hued clouds in the distance, whereas before her view was mainly of the kitchen floor. What a surprise when, on Christmas day, she could see the partridges that walked across the top of the stone wall surrounding her garden!

With a sudden drop of temperatures in the new year, Carina convinced Lydia and the Maestro to mete out some of the remaining finances received from the sale of the Sienese Duchess's ring to embellish the normal skimpy fare at her Sunday lunch with more hearty culinary dishes. She wanted to keep her friends well nourished. Lydia helped Carina get all the ingredients for ribollita and pappa al pomodoro, a rich tomato and bread soup. Sister Clara helped by ordering from the baker a special panettone for Carina's guests, and the thought of showering her friends with special delicacies gave Carina great satisfaction. When that Sunday arrived, she sang as she adorned the large table in the kitchen with garlands of the last autumn leaves from her backyard garden.

During the same time of year, the Sienese ducal family returned to Florence for more discussions regarding Massimo's future marriage to Donatella, and the unveiling of the Maestro's portraits of Massimo and Donatella. Lydia, Carina, Pietro, and the Maestro's apprentices all observed the creation of these portraits. They admired the Maestro's artistry in both portraits, which glowed with his insight into his subjects and his expert painterly skill. He captured the noble gentleness which defined Massimo by placing the young duke in a pastoral scene. Surrounded by his hunting dogs, Massimo gestured towards them in appreciation of their fidelity. As anticipated, he accentuated the Duke's garments with the gold leaf he had purchased with the sale of the Duke's mother's ring. The unexpected gleams of gold gave a regal aspect to the portrait. When it came to the young Duchess, the Maestro portrayed her in shimmering dancing attire. Bouquets of flowers graced the background as Donatella beamed, all reflected in the Maestro's choice of a color palette of rosy pinks and lavenders.

The morning after the Sienese ducal family arrived to Lucrezia's palazzo, Massimo forayed on horseback out into the countryside with several of his attendants, and as it turned out, they headed up to Settignano. Realizing his proximity to the Maestro's Studio, Massimo decided to pay a cordial visit, even though it was a Sunday and he was previously unannounced.

A knocking on the main door caught their attention as Carina and Lydia made the final touches to the dishes to be presented at the banquet table (which was, in reality, Lydia's kitchen table). Carina knew the knock on the front door was not from one of her guests, because they always trooped in through the kitchen's side door. The Maestro himself went to open the door, and was surprised to discover Duke Massimo, now dismounted from his horse, and his attendants remaining on horseback. The Maestro had warm feelings for the Duke, remembering him as a young man of gentle character, and he invited Massimo inside. Except for his closest valet, Massimo excused his riding attendants to return to Florence to let his family know he might be late for their midday meal at Duchess Lucrezia's palazzo.

A few steps into the Maestro's home and Massimo paused, aware of the joyful sounds coming from the kitchen and the delicious aromas. "I have interrupted your Sunday meal; I am so sorry."

"Not at all," said the Maestro. "As you may remember, our Carina prepares a special luncheon for her needy friends every Sunday. We made the decision today to use some of the funds from your family's generous donation of the rings, so Carina has truly prepared a feast this time." The Maestro paused and then, taking note of the curious expression on the young Duke's face, he invited Massimo to join them in the kitchen. "There is always room for one more at our humble banquet table."

Carina stood astonished in the middle of the kitchen when she saw Massimo. She felt both intimidated by the young Duke's presence and delighted because he would see the fruits of his family's kind donation toward this event. He seemed even more handsome than she had recalled, but what struck her most was the kind manner in which he greeted her rag-tag group of friends. When he complemented her on the pasta al pomodoro dish, saying it was the most delicious he had ever tasted, she felt her cheeks flush. Surely everyone noticed.

After the pots of soup and pasta and the panettone had been devoured and when all her friends looked satiated, Carina picked up her dulcimer and Sister Clara picked up her guitar and the two of them played a lively tune. Unable to resist the music, Carina's friends whirled and twirled and Massimo — generous, kind Massimo — danced with Lydia, and now it was her turn to blush!

Later that evening there would be dancing in Lucrezia's palazzo as well. As a trio of musicians strummed their lutes and their piccolo instruments, the aristocracy of Florence danced their slow formal pavane processional. Massimo watched from the corner of the vast hall with a pensive expression. This was the family that his fortune would be tied with. Arranged marriages were the norm. It was his duty to advance his family's standing, but the impending nuptials weighed heavy on his heart. Having just earlier that day been a guest at Carina's beggars' banquet, Massimo was struck by the contrasting opulence, the silver platters piled high with roasted pheasants, the glint of jewels around necks and on garments. Why was it that encountering the ragtag gathering at the Studio with their meal of humble fare had given him more joy than this evening? He was relieved that the next day he would be returning to Siena to continue his education in philosophy and history in his own household. He felt tired and longed for the evening to be over.

He was pulled out of his ruminations when the music suddenly stopped. Lucrezia and her younger son Duke Eduardo stood in the center of the hall while servants carried in the Maestro's two veiled portraits of Donatella and Massimo. They placed each of the portraits on easels and stepped aside. With a flourish, Lucrezia unveiled them.

Donatella rushed forward to look at her portrait as Lucrezia beckoned for Massimo to join her. There was no denying the Maestro's artistry. There was also no denying the lack of chemistry between Donatella and Massimo. Whispered remarks were exchanged amongst the guests, along with the enthusiastic clapping of hands. There would be the formality of a long courtship, and of course everyone knew it was the celebration of an attempt for a political alliance, organized to strengthen the Principality of Tuscany, as the House of Florence now dominated the House of Siena.

Chapter Fifteen

Every six months, as instructed by Doctor Benedetto, the Maestro adjusted Carina's brace so as to force her back into a new position, more upright. It was difficult to endure. The brace only came off at night, and Lydia helped her put it back on in the morning. Carina appreciated the doctor and his gentle manner when he came to check her progress. That is, until he reached into his satchel and brought out the tonics he brewed for her, little bottles of dreadful tasting liquid that he insisted she drink in his presence.

"Will it help?" she always asked.

His response was always an enthusiastic, "Yes!"

In the midst of all of this, Carina's dedication to the practice of embroidery and the interweaving of delicate stitches taught to her by Sister Clara became her refuge. The intricacies and beauty of her tapestries became so sophisticated that women came to buy them as decoration for their homes, and they commissioned pieces to be sown into their clothing. Carina added artistic beading to her embroideries, learning from the Maestro's inspired sense of light and color. Aware of how important the embroidery was to Carina, the Maestro gladly drew the backgrounds upon which she applied her silk threads and iridescent beads. She used the monies received from the sale of her embroideries towards funding her Sunday dinner gatherings. This continued to be her utmost source of joy, a light in her personal painful world.

As always, the Maestro managed to find ways to use Carina as a model in his paintings because of the beautiful features of her countenance. She spent many hours in the Studio posing as the angel in his "Annunciation" painting. Her brace was hidden by her usual sack-like dress, but that did not diminish the discomfort she felt as she posed on one knee with her hand extended. She hid her pain well, and the Maestro, absorbed in his work, was not aware when her breathing became labored. Carina told herself that posing for the Maestro was the least service she could do for him, but on one particularly cold day, when the look in her eyes was uncharacteristically bleak, she was unable to sustain her pose a second longer and she dropped her head and cried out in pain as she sunk to both knees. The Maestro immediately stopped his work. Pietro, who had also been sketching Carina and standing closer to her than the Maestro, quietly derided her as an unsuitable model, shielding his harsh words by turning his back to the Maestro, who would decidedly disapprove of him.

The Maestro helped Carina to her feet.

"Pietro, please help her back to her room."

Carina slowly made her way back to her room where she fell into her bed and hid under the covers and pillows.

Carina had reached one of those moments of unbearable exhaustion, when her goal to be free from the bondage of deformity felt impossible. This was not the first time Carina had faced an urgent need for healing and strength. She was familiar with the experience of feeling spent and utterly defeated. But this was only temporary. She had learned to be patient, to wait, and to prayerfully trust the Lord to give her the strength and encouragement to rally. God's promise, "I will never leave you nor forsake you," resonated in her heart. Carina bowed her head and quietly spoke, "Thank you, Jesus. Yes, Lord, I receive your love and grace. I refuse to harbor fear and self-pity. Please shed light on the dark places within me." Carina prayed to be delivered from her difficulties.

Carina understood the holy scripture, "Ask and you shall receive." As she prayed to be released from bondage, she believed in the Lord's ability and merciful love to heal her. She looked within, so as to receive the abundance that comes when peace replaces distress, when soundness replaces instability, when love is exchanged for fear. Thus, Carina was released into a restorative slumber, transformed to a place of assurance where she knew she had prayerfully sought help, and indeed she had been heard, and it was coming from the Living God.

Chapter Sixteen

Two years had passed, and Carina's strength and stature increased. Because the Maestro set up Carina's embroidery loom in a well-lit corner of the Studio, she shared the company of the Maestro's apprentices while they were doing their sketches and painting. When Carina would tire and need a break from the stress of working with her back brace on, she would stop her embroidery and strum and hum on her dulcimer which she kept close by. She made such sensitive music that all in the Studio enjoyed it and did not consider her dulcimer playing an intrusion.

Pietro was working on a portrait commission of an important Florentine noble lady; she and her husband had asked Pietro to paint her as Mary with the baby Jesus so they could place the painting in the chapel of their palazzo. Carina observed that Pietro was struggling with this piece of artwork. Even though he had done all the necessary sketches of the noble lady, he kept changing his ideas for the composition, eliminating them over and over. The painting only included the Madonna and Child, seated in the actual chapel, with little else. It seemed to Carina that he needed more elements.

With great diplomacy, she asked Pietro, "I see you are doing a portrait with the Madonna and Child. Have you thought about adding the presence of an angel?"

"An angel?" responded Pietro.

"Yes, surely there were angels attending the Madonna and Child!"

Piero looked back and forth between her and his stalled painting. Carina could tell that he was entertaining the idea, and with an unprecedented boldness, she asked Pietro if he would like her to pose for him as the angel.

Pietro hesitated for a moment, but he realized that her offer could very much help him. "Well, yes, Carina, thank you. Do you have the energy to pose for a while now so I can see what ideas come forth?"

Carina put down her embroidery needle and slipped out of her chair. Pietro moved the chair to a good place for posing, and Carina took her position. She was still holding her dulcimer which she placed in her lap. As she started to put the dulcimer down, Pietro asked, "Do you think an angel could be playing a heavenly instrument similar to your dulcimer?"

"I would hope so!"

Pietro posed Carina with her dulcimer on her lap and began to sketch her into the composition, the corners of his mouth soon turning up into a smile as he worked. Carina made herself available to Pietro over a period of time, and his problematic portrait blossomed into a strong and original composition. Everyone in the Studio observed this unfolding, including the Maestro, and they encouraged Pietro, complementing him. And so, after years of tension between Pietro and Carina, there was a transformation in their relationship, and Pietro treated her with dignity and respect from that time forth.

Meanwhile, the happy day came when Carina embroidered the last few stitches on her most ambitious project, a scene from "The Angel Releasing Peter from Chains in

Prison." She had just turned seventeen, and for the last year she had been working diligently on this work of art. The Maestro had helped, as usual, by drawing the background on the embroidery canvas, but it was her intricate stitching and beadwork, and her devotion and commitment to the subject of the tapestry that brought the scene to life.

Setting down one of the long embroidery needles that she used, she sat back to admire her work. It pleased her. Rising from her chair, she headed to the kitchen where she found Lydia making ravioli with artichokes.

"Lydia, it's done!"

Lydia clapped her hands in excitement and followed Carina back to the Studio, where she admired the tapestry and the delicate beading of the angel's wings that created a rainbow of glowing colors. The Maestro appeared and congratulated Carina on her dedication and artistry. Even Pietro, who had heard the joyful voices, appeared and complemented her. Lydia put her arm gently and lovingly around Carina's shoulders, over the straps of the heavy brace. "Have you decided where you would like to place the tapestry?"

"Signora della Grazia has offered to purchase it. It will bring in even more money for—"

Lydia interrupted, "I know, I know, for your friends and the Sunday banquet, but maybe this is one you keep. You deserve beauty and abundance for yourself."

"Stop," Carina said with a smile. "I already have that."

"Yes, you do, and I also wish for you to meet a handsome young man."

"Oh, my goodness!" Carina was blushing. Recently Lydia had started talking to her about the young men in Settignano, and Carina too had started to notice them.

The two women made their way to the room they still shared. It was overcrowded with a spare brace and parts for her loom, and the walls were adorned with tapestries Carina had created when she first started — simple but beautiful scenes of nature and floral arrangements with flowers from her garden. There was still space above Carina's bed, and that was where they worked on hanging the tapestry. What a satisfaction and accomplishment for Carina.

After hanging the tapestry, Lydia told Carina the news that she had been keeping secret all day. Doctor Benedetto was coming to visit Carina for an evaluation of her progress. If all was well, she would be relieved of the brace.

"Really?" Carina looked pensive, as if she were not sure this day would actually arrive.

"The doctor sent word to the Maestro. He will be joining us for lunch."

Within the hour the doctor arrived, and Lydia led him to the bedroom, where he removed the brace and examined Carina and asked her to perform a range of motions. He then smiled and remarked on her outstanding progress.

Carina remained upright, holding onto a chair.

"Carina," he said. "Do you feel any pain?"

She shook her head. "No."

"Then you are done wearing the brace every day. From now on you will wear it every second day for several months, and then not at all, depending on how you feel. Continue to take it off at night when you sleep. There is a caveat. At the first sign of fatigue or pain, it goes back on immediately." The doctor went ahead to join the Maestro in the Studio. He was a few steps down the passageway when he noticed Carina was not following him. He hurried back. "Carina!

Join us. You can walk without the brace." He took Carina's hand and gently guided her as she took her first tentative steps upright without the brace.

Her steps resembled that of a gangly fawn. Freed from the encumbrance and weight of the brace, she felt almost giddy, light as a feather, and she could not stop smiling as she walked towards her beloved Maestro. He had now entered into the golden years of his life, and although his demeanor was careful and controlled, he remained agile. His gray hair, flowing beard and commanding stature gave him the appearance of a prophet, an approachable and unintimidating prophet.

His eyes filled with tears and his hands trembled as he reflected on the arduous, courageous struggle that Carina had endured. And then he too began to smile as his beloved little girl, who had become a gracious and beautiful woman, approached him.

After a delicious lunch with Doctor Benedetto, they bid him farewell, and Carina and the Maestro returned to the Studio. Carina seated herself carefully on the model's platform, took a deep breath and gave a sigh of relief, looking at the Maestro. This would be the first day she would pose without a brace.

"Are you ready?" he asked.

Carina nodded with a careful, "Yes."

The Maestro and Carina settled into their familiar way of rapport. As Carina held her pose, her eyes viewed the tapestries of her own that the Maestro had hung in his workspace. A surge of newfound energy coursed through her being. Her freedom from the brace was surely a miracle, and the warmth and love she felt for the Maestro, Lydia, the doctor, her ragtag friends of the beggars' banquet — oh, how she couldn't wait for them to see her — almost felt overwhelming. The Maestro lifted his brush and daubed it on the palette. The small portrait of Carina that he was working on now reflected the harmony, goodness, and grace she embodied. With each delicate brushstroke he brought forth the pensive depth in her face, and he surrounded her with a crystalline atmosphere of almost solidified light.

They took a break, and Carina turned her head to stretch and caught sight of one of Pietro's portraits that he had recently put on display. It captured the beauty of a young noble lady with a cloud of red hair and bold blue eyes. This was another commissioned portrait of the Duchess Donatella that Duchess Lucrezia had asked the Maestro to do. But because the Maestro was already working on several commissioned paintings, he asked Pietro to paint the portrait. Pietro very willingly agreed and went several times to their palazzo to do sketches of Donatella. Pietro had become an accomplished artist in the tradition of the Maestro, and this portrait was one of his finest. Some might even consider him a great artist. Carina then looked at the other side of the Studio where two of the Maestro's great masterpieces, "Leda and the Swan," and the "Madonna and Child with St. Anne," stood humbly on easels pushed into corners. Carina had posed for both of those as well.

Resuming their work, they bantered easily. The Maestro congratulated her on her achievements, both in the physical and artistic realms, directing their conversation toward the future. Carina was tender with the Maestro, modest and somewhat wistful. He asked her if she has been praying for a beloved. And just as she had with Lydia, she flushed and told him she had not received the faith to pray for such a thing yet.

Chapter Seventeen

About three months before the planned wedding of Massimo and Donatella, when both the Maestro and Pietro were working on their current and most important commissioned paintings, the harmony at the Studio was abruptly interrupted by a loud knock on the front door. Lydia, who had been in the kitchen, gathered her skirts around her and went to open the door. She was surprised by unannounced visitors, but recognizing the Florentine noble family of the Duchess Lucrezia, she welcomed them. High-pitched voices of women filled the passageway as Lucrezia and Anna, Donatella, and her mother, Duchess Francesca, followed by a retinue of attendants, flooded into the Studio. Carina immediately recognized the subject of Pietro's portrait. Donatella stood in the middle of the Studio dazzling everyone with her billowing hair and her grandiosely fashioned outfit. Jewels cascaded all over the petite duchess, who was just under five feet tall. But her stature belied her confidence, and she immediately took command of the occasion, ordering about her ladies-in-waiting.

Surprised by this unexpected, even rude, intrusion by the ducal nobility, the Maestro stopped painting and slowly stood to bow to the noble family. Lydia curtsied deeply, but Carina found herself in an awkward situation. She rose out of her chair on the modeling platform, and having grown quite tall, she towered above Donatella. Being without her back brace, she felt unsure of her ability to lean over, but she took courage and carefully managed a graceful little curtsy.

"A seat for my grandmother and mother," Donatella instructed Pietro.

Carina quietly observed the unfolding scene while Pietro placed two chairs in the center of the Studio. She had a faint memory of the ducal family passing her in the street a decade ago when she and the Maestro and Lydia had made their way to the cathedral for the June celebration of San Giovanni. Then she recalled the portraits of Duke Massimo and Duchess Donatella that the Maestro had painted years ago, and the humiliation she had felt when the family had visited the Studio and Donatella shrieked when she saw her in the water closet. Duchess Lucrezia's strident voice had cut through the air then, but now she spoke with a slight tremor. The Duchess used a gilded cane, and as she took a seat Carina noticed how her hands shook. Behind her stood a woman with an obsequious demeanor who Carina remembered as being her servant. Anna, yes, that was her name.

Flustered by this unexpected visit, Pietro barked orders at Lydia to prepare refreshments. He hovered around Donatella and her grandmother as they admired his portraiture.

"My dear granddaughter looks very beautiful, Pietro. The ducal Sienese family will surely approve," offered Lucrezia.

Donatella's mother chimed in, "The ducal Sienese family will be arriving soon, and we wanted to view your portrait of Donatella beforehand. We intend to present it to Duke Massimo as part of our upcoming wedding festivities."

Carina had not heard mention of Duke Massimo's name for some time, but the warm feelings of affection she felt for him after his last visit remained. She glanced again at the young Duchess. How fortunate she was to be betrothed to such a noble and kind man.

Lucrezia called out to Anna, who immediately stepped around to help steady her mistress on her feet. Leaning on her cane, Lucrezia moved from one of the Maestro's masterpieces to the next. But it was Carina's embroidery work that seemed to delight her the most.

"Maestro, I did not know that you worked in the medium of embroidery and beadwork."

The Maestro explained, "These beautiful tapestries are by Carina. I only help her by painting the background on her embroidery canvases."

"Carina?" enquired Lucrezia.

Lydia interjected, pointing to Carina who had quietly seated herself once again in the chair on the Maestro's modeling platform. "Yes, Carina lives with us, and she is an accomplished embroideress."

Lucrezia admired another unfinished piece of Carina's embroidery displayed on a loom. Sensing an opportunity for financial opportunity, Lydia said, "Her tapestries are appreciated by many of the fine ladies of Settignano and Florence, and Carina also does embroidery for their important garments and gowns. She has been inspired by the Maestro to the highest level of artistry."

The Maestro added even more words of enthusiasm. "Perhaps the Duchesses would like to see more examples of Carina's exquisite tapestry work. I am sure she would be honored to show you more of her finished pieces which are displayed in her bedchamber behind the kitchen."

Considering Donatella's upcoming marriage and the need for a lavish wardrobe that would leave an impression on the nobility of Florence, Lucrezia announced that they should view the tapestries, and she instructed Donatella to join her and Anna.

"Oh please, Nonna, no!" Donatella stood rigid. Now it was her turn to remember how several years ago she'd been horrified to run into a deformed child in the water closet. "Please, I don't want to go back there."

"If someone escorts me, I will choose some examples of the work to bring into the Studio to display for the Duchesses Lucrezia, Francesca and Donatella," said Anna.

"An excellent idea," said the Maestro, and he instructed Pietro to do so.

Pietro would have preferred the attention to remain on his portrait of Donatella, but he led the way through the kitchen to the bedroom. He and Anna gingerly reconnoitered around the crowded bedroom, while Lydia and Carina watched from the doorway. Pietro pointed to the pieces hanging on the walls and asked which ones Anna thought would be suitable to show to Lucrezia. Anna, however, was momentarily taken by the braces stacked against the wall.

"What is the use of all this paraphernalia?" she enquired.

Pietro explained that these contraptions were examples of the Maestro's genius for inventions. "He and Doctor Benedetto developed all of these therapeutic materials to assist Carina in her transformation."

"What form of transformation?" Anna asked.

"Carina was born with severe physical deformities. We all think it is a miracle that she even survived."

Anna who'd been inspecting the embroideries, lending half an ear to Pietro, now turned to look at him. "A physical deformity?"

Pietro told how he had bravely saved Carina as a newborn infant from an unsavory situation and certain death when he whisked her from abandonment in the central plaza of Settignano into the arms of the Maestro.

Anna's shrewd eyes moved from Carina's rich embroidery, depicting her freedom from bondage, displayed on the wall, to the contraptions which Carina had used to receive healing.

Carina had been told before about how she had been discovered abandoned in the Piazza of Settignano. The story often gave her comfort because of the loving home she had been given. To her the story had a blessed ending, and she couldn't imagine living in a more welcome refuge. But listening to Pietro's retelling of her private history, a nervousness overcame her, and she reached for the old shawl on the chair close to the door.

Anna turned to look at Carina. There was a particular beauty to Carina's countenance that resembled the gentle features of Duchess Grazia. Then she recognized the well-worn shawl that Carina had draped across her shoulders. It was Anna's shawl, the one with embroidered tiny blue flowers, given to Anna by Lucrezia many years ago. It was the shawl that Anna had, out of desperation, used to swaddled Carina on the first day of her life.

Anna stood there stricken. The child she thought she had eliminated appeared to be standing in front of her, alive and well and restored in body. Anna remembered her countless tormenting nightmares, focused on her abandoning Carina in the piazza. She had spent years privately thrashing over her actions. Had she exercised compassion by refusing to murder Duchess Grazia's deformed child at the demand of

Duchess Lucrezia, or was she guilty of a lack of moral courage when she dumped the helpless child in a bundle and left her to an uncertain destiny?

At first, Anna's face had barely revealed what was going through her mind. Now her expression changed. Her lips pursed, her brow furrowed, and her eyes narrowed. She needed to protect herself. What was done was done. The most immediate concern was Duchess Donatella's wedding looming ahead, and Anna was determined that nothing should interrupt that.

Choosing to ignore Carina, she turned to Lydia who was also silently observing the scene. "Is this all true?"

Lydia simply nodded her head in a confirming yes.

Anna felt panic, but being accustomed to the pressures of court life, she took a deep breath to compose herself. She would improvise a plan to keep the knowledge of these facts from Duchess Lucrezia. She quickly chose the best tapestries to show to Lucrezia and Donatella and ordered Pietro to bring them into the Studio.

Easels were commandeered into place and Pietro and even the Maestro draped the tapestries over them. Anna lauded the virtues of Carina's craftsmanship, winning over Lucrezia and Francesca's admiration with her flattery for Carina. Even Pietro joined in the tide of appreciation.

A smile came over Lucrezia's countenance while she carefully examined each piece of Carina's embroidery. Her eyes lit up. "Do you not think that adding the handiwork of this embroideress could enhance Donatella's wedding vestment?"

Anna took in a sharp breath, amazed that Lucrezia had just put into motion the very scheme that had entered Anna's mind.

"That could be all right, Nonna," said Donatella, "but is she good enough? Can she work with pearls? The cache of pearls we want to use should arrive from Venice any day now."

Stepping in, the Maestro reassured the young duchess that Carina was exceptionally skilled.

For several minutes Lucrezia and Donatella bantered back and forth about pearls — how many were to be used and could they get more and what if the shipment were delayed? They were due to arrive, but how would the seamstresses already working on her wedding dress be able to make adjustments?

Duchess Francesca, who had stepped aside to admire another tapestry, held it to the light and swayed it gently from side to side. "Look!"

The silver and white beads sparkling and dancing in the light drew Donatella closer. "And with the pearls I will have the finest wedding in all of Florence!" she exclaimed.

Lucrezia tapped her gilded cane on the floor and promptly drew everyone's attention. "We would like the girl to work on Duchess Donatella's wedding vestments."

Carina shuddered. Somehow she sensed there was a darkness to this offer. But the Maestro and Lydia seemed delighted with the invitation, and Carina tried to shrug free of her doubts.

"You are being recognized for your talent," the Maestro said. "It is an honor to be offered this commission. And from the noble family of Florence. Think of it, Carina!"

A lull settled on the Studio. It had been decided, but then Anna stepped forward with another request. "This type of embroidery work simply must take place within the palazzo. Surely you understand that we cannot bring the wedding dress here. There needs to be collaboration with the other embroideresses already working on the trousseau."

Anna spoke to Lucrezia. "Would it not be best that she stay at the palazzo for the duration of the work? She can start tomorrow."

The Maestro, Lydia and Carina all took a deep breath at once and exchanged concerned glances. With all eyes on Carina, Anna ventured, "This is such a wonderful opportunity for you!"

The details were finalized, and Pietro committed to return the following day, Sunday, to help escort Carina into Florence.

Echoing what Anna had said, Lucrezia spoke emphatically to Carina. "This is a great honor. I trust you understand. You will stay in the servants' quarters at the palazzo. Donatella's dress will require many fittings and alterations, and you will become part of a collaborative team of seamstresses. It is absolutely necessary that you are there until the wedding day."

Carina's move away from the Studio was a cause for concern because of her still-delicate physical condition. She had progressed remarkably, and the last thing Lydia wanted was a setback. Lydia expressed her worries, but Anna craftily assured everyone that the move would be to Carina's advantage. She attempted to allay all fears by promising to also care for Carina herself personally. "If you give me the instructions regarding her physical therapy needs, I will be sure to follow them."

Lydia thanked her profusely, and all concerns were forgotten. Both she and the Maestro had wanted this for Carina, a fulfilling life within society. Carina would be exposed to many new acquaintances, and her horizons would expand from this experience in the palazzo. Anna adroitly added that by working with other great seamstresses in the field of embroidery, Carina would develop important professional contacts. It would only enhance her reputation as a craftsman to participate in the embroidery of Donatella's prestigious wedding trousseau.

Events unfolded rapidly, and with the chatter back and forth in the Studio, no one noticed that Carina had excused herself to return to her room. She sat alone on her bed pallet, examining the walls, now unadorned in the places where they had been stripped of her tapestries. Carina, like Anna, stared at her back brace, knowing that it had taken on a new and important dimension in her life — different from what it had meant earlier that morning. Somehow Carina sensed that she had been violated, and yet she could not discern what was troubling her. She shivered and reached for the shawl with the blue cornflowers that always gave her comfort. She wrapped it around her shoulders, pulling it tight. Was there something wrong with her? Why was she not rejoicing at her invitation into the very palazzo itself?

Chapter Eighteen

The next morning Carina and Lydia alternated between organizing Carina's things to take to the palazzo and preparing the customary beggars' banquet. Carina, as always, was happy to see her guests. She greeted Solomon, Sara, Stefano, Rodolfo, Amelia who was still unable to speak, Samson, Adamo, and Delmonico, who was accompanied, as usual, by Sister Clara, as his eyesight was so poor. Only Maria was missing, as she had passed away.

Today was particularly special because Don Paolo, the priest of their parish and close friend of the Maestro, was back from his travels to Rome, and Carina knew he would make a special effort to attend the lunch. Don Paolo often met with the Maestro; they were both scholars who studied the holy scriptures and worked to translate them from Latin to the Italian vernacular.

This was also the first time that Carina participated without her back brace, and her dear friends rejoiced at her ongoing liberation. They ate heartily, and Don Paolo complimented her on the delicious dishes she had prepared. But Carina's mind was elsewhere. After partaking hastily of the meal, she regretfully informed her guests that she had to leave. "My dear beloved friends, I need to pack and prepare to go to Duchess Lucrezia's palazzo this evening, because I have been given an assignment there as an embroideress!"

After expressing their happiness at Carina's news, her ragtag group of friends started to leave. Lydia spoke up. "Please, remain and finish lunch with the Maestro and Don Paolo and Sister Clara, while I help Carina. When we are ready, then you can help us gather everything and send Carina on her way!"

Lydia and Carina retreated to the bedroom to finish putting together her necessary belongings. This included fitting Carina's back brace on, as she would surely need it to endure the trip into Florence. Carina's tenderhearted family of guests got into action and excitedly pitched in to help. Sister Clara did her best to make the organization process orderly, but a joyful chaos prevailed. Spools of runaway embroidery thread raced here and there, chased by Buono and Buona, while Adamo carried the unwieldy loom to Samuele's cart. Stefano adorned Golden Slippers' harness with flowers from the garden.

Amidst this impromptu air of celebration, Carina continued to ponder the inexplicable sense of trepidation she harbored. She clutched her dulcimer. Lydia had questioned whether she should take it, thinking surely she would be too busy to play. But Carina was loathe to leave it behind, knowing she would need comforting music to encourage her.

Pietro arrived, remembering his commitment from the previous day to escort Carina into Florence.

With the loom safely loaded in the cart, Adamo excused himself to return to his work in the Duomo bell tower. He needed to ring the bells to announce the expected arrival of the Sienese royal contingent that evening. Before bent-over Adamo departed, he reminded Carina that once they both had been in the same physical condition, and he encouraged her with the assurance that, because she had developed so far, surely she would continue to meet with success.

"Coraggio!" he proclaimed.

After tender moments with her two dogs, Carina tearfully kissed the Maestro, Lydia, Sister Clara and her beloved friends goodbye. The Maestro asked Don Paolo if he would pray a special blessing over Carina. They all joined hands and Don Paolo prayed for Carina, and recited Psalm 23:

> The LORD is my shepherd; I shall not want.
> He maketh me to lie down in green pastures:
>   he leadeth me beside the still waters.
> He restoreth my soul: he leadeth me in the
>   paths of righteousness for his name's sake.
> Yea, though I walk through the valley of the
>   shadow of death, I will fear no evil: for
>   thou art with me; thy rod and thy staff
>   they comfort me.
> Thou preparest a table before me in the
>   presence of mine enemies: thou anointest
>   my head with oil; my cup runneth over.
> Surely goodness and mercy shall follow me
>   all the days of my life: and I will dwell in
>   the house of the LORD forever.

"Look!" cried Sara as Don Paolo concluded his prayer. A kaleidoscope of swallowtail butterflies borne on a light breeze fluttered around them. Carina mounted up onto her seat in the overloaded cart. Samuele flicked the reins, Golden Slippers stepped forward, and Pietro, astride his horse, led the way to Florence and the palazzo. Before being lost from view, Carina turned and called out to her friends, waving goodbye, "I promise to come back next Sunday for our banquet together! I have not abandoned you!"

Carina sat quiet and pensive as they descended the hillside, with the top-heavy cart lurching perilously around the curves. Several times Pietro glanced back at her and even reassured her that this was indeed a remarkable opportunity. Still, her feelings of fear persisted. After some time, they reached the long driveway leading to Lucrezia's ducal palazzo. Samuele had to jockey for space with other carriages also heading toward the palazzo; Carina's arrival coincided with the much-anticipated entrance of the Grand Duke of Siena and his family, inaugurating several weeks of pre-wedding festivities.

Carina caught a glimpse of the ornate ducal carriage and Massimo's fine profile as it passed by. Her feelings of immense gratitude towards him briefly replaced the growing unease she felt at this request to stay at the palazzo. The young Duke's generous gift of his ring to her had commenced her journey of liberation from deep-set physical bondage. She'd been too shy to properly thank him when he came to her beggars' banquet two years ago, but she vowed that if by chance she ran into him at the palazzo, she would do so.

The tree-lined road widened and forked as they reached the palazzo, and with a gentle click of his tongue and a nudge with the harness reins, Samuele urged Golden Slippers to the left, where they found the palazzo's side entrance for tradesmen and deliveries.

The servant attending the tradesmen's entrance went to find Anna while Carina and Samuele waited. Pietro, having seen the Duke of Siena's carriage, bid his farewell to Carina and made his way to the front of the palazzo where he rather brashly approached Duke Massimo to reintroduce himself. And then, without permission and wanting to impress Massimo with his artistic bravura, Pietro invited Massimo to come to the Maestro's Studio to view his portrait of the Duchess Donatella. Massimo graciously agreed to come, for he welcomed an opportunity to see the Maestro again.

Unbeknownst to all those below, Donatella and Lucrezia had also witnessed the ducal carriage's arrival from a balustrade overlooking the courtyard. Observing Massimo's reserved demeanor, Donatella frowned and sighed heavily. "I just wish he were livelier. He seems like an old man!"

"Old man?" Lucrezia objected. "He is a handsome youth and a nobleman!" Interrupting the potentially heated conversation between grandmother and granddaughter, the Duomo belfry tolled loudly, heralding the arrival of the Sienese ducal family. Somehow the bells did not sound full of joyful portent, but instead resonated with a ponderous tone.

In the rear of the palazzo the narrow corridors were dimly lit. Carina followed Anna up one staircase and round another — the journey seemed endless — until they reached the third floor. Anna had not spoken another word to Carina, who felt increasingly intimidated by her ominous presence. Finally, they reached a small chamber.

"Your belongings will arrive shortly. My quarters are next door," Anna said curtly. "I will be keeping in close contact with you so as to give you your instructions."

A young porter soon arrived with Carina's possessions.

"You must be tired from all the excitement," Anna continued. "The work starts tomorrow, but for now I suggest you have dinner in your room. I'll arrange for it to be brought up."

The stale air of the room, the small, barred window, the long and confusing walk up the stairs and down endless passageways; suddenly it was all too much for Carina, and she buckled. Alarmed, Anna led her to the bed and insisted that she help Carina take off her back brace, so that she could be more comfortable. With trembling hands, Anna loosened one buckle after another, freeing Carina from the very thing that could imprison Anna herself. Anna propped Carina's back brace against the wall, shuddering with her own sense of fear and trepidation, wondering if she would receive her just due in this life or go to her grave with the hideous secrets hidden in her heart. Then, without another look at Carina, she hurriedly left the room and locked the door behind her.

Slumped on the bed in her dreary chamber, Carina ached with longing for all that she had left behind — the smells from the kitchen as Lydia cooked dinner, the companionship of Buono and Buona, the colors of the paintings that adorned the walls, the way the sunlight caught the shimmering beads in her tapestries. She missed the love and laughter that was such a hallmark of her life with her adopted family. She missed the company of the Maestro's apprentices at the Studio, and she even missed Pietro, a familiar, yet sometimes grumpy face.

The sounds of movement from the courtyard below drew her to the small window in her room and she looked down, grasping the window bars to steady herself. The excitement created by Duke Massimo's arrival filtering up through the courtyard made her situation even more intolerable. Seeing him after such a long time stirred up a myriad of emotions within her. Wanting to quell her feelings, Carina wished she could just sleep forever. She'd worked so hard to achieve healing and regain her stature, but now she had to acknowledge she'd been motivated by a secret longing. She had been dreaming of Massimo. To be frustrated while working toward a goal is difficult, but to have achieved that goal and have it turn out to be an empty, useless achievement, is worse. Carina reexamined her life of hard work. For what purpose? To what end? To be ultimately defeated because she could never achieve total fulfillment? Her dream of having a love of her own now seemed dim, an unattainable desire.

She turned to her dulcimer. She had been wise to bring it. That sweet familiar instrument, made for her with love, would soothe her. She took her dulcimer out of the protective case she had made for it, tuned it up and began to strum and sing to herself:

> I am trusting you, oh Lord,
> To lift up my heavy burdens.
> I am trusting you, oh Lord,
> To touch my life and set me free.
>
> The question is do I believe you,
> To do the things you say you do?
> I am remembering your faithfulness,
> How in the past you saw me through!
>
> E se io non vedo te, (And if I cannot see you)
> So che tu vedi me, (I know you can see me)
> E se sono triste sai, (And if I am sad)
> So che tu mi solleverai (I know that you will
>   lift me up)

Io mi fido in te, Signor, (I am trusting you, oh Lord)
Di portarmi nella gioia, (To carry me into joy)
Io mi fido in te, Signor, (I am trusting you, oh Lord)
Di portarmi nel tuo amor (To carry me in your love)

I am trusting you, oh Lord,
To lift up my heavy burdens.
I am trusting you, oh Lord,
To touch my life and set me free.

The sound of music entertaining the guests at the welcoming party for the Grand Duke of Siena drifted up to Carina's lonely chamber and joined the gentle strumming of her dulcimer as if in harmony and gave Carina comfort. Once again, she felt reassured of God's love for her and at peace, buoyed in her faith.

In the richly decorated rooms of the palazzo the throng of noble guests were immersed in glamor and glitter. Duchess Lucrezia had instructed her staff to prepare a magnificent reception, and the alluring aroma of the delicious food preparations spread throughout the entire palazzo. Everyone seemed to be enjoying themselves, except for the soon-to-be-wedded young couple. The guests soon took their seats in the banquet hall. At the head of the main table sat Duchess Lucrezia, with her sons Duke Onorio and Duke Eduardo to the left and right of her. Duke Eduardo's wife and Duchess Donatella and the guests of honor, the Duke and Duchess of Siena and Duke Massimo, were seated on either side. Massimo had been the last to arrive to his assigned seat because he had again been admiring the artistry in all the details around the palazzo. And just as he had with his earlier visit, he found the evening events and the conversation lacking. His parents had urged him to make a show of participating with more liveliness, and he complied with diplomacy, but half-heartedly. What fascinated Massimo more than the festivities spread out before him, was the display of paintings on the walls. He recognized the Maestro's masterpieces, including "The Annunciation," "Leda and the Swan," and the "Madonna and Child with St. Anne" and gazed unabashedly at these paintings, for which Carina had been the model. It became apparent that he was paying undue attention to the display on the walls, as opposed to the display at the table, much to the consternation of Donatella, who glowered.

Chapter Nineteen

*E*arly the next morning Carina was awakened by a shaft of sunlight beaming through her small bedchamber window. Her day would have typically begun with a series of stretches prescribed by Doctor Benedetto, but feeling pressure to be ready at a moment's notice, all thoughts of any therapeutic routine were abandoned.

Anna arrived carrying Carina's breakfast, and once again, Anna's hands trembled uncharacteristically. She watched Carina eat and then helped Carina into her back brace to support herself for the day's work.

She then escorted Carina to the workroom where she introduced Carina to the seamstresses and the two embroideresses who were toiling on Donatella's wardrobe for her wedding trousseau. The fiery-haired young duchess was in the midst of a fitting, and she barely registered Carina's presence.

"Oh stop! You're pinching me!" Donatella complained. "I hope all this pricking and squeezing me is worth it."

Carina found the activity in the workroom mesmerizing: some of the finest seamstresses devoted to their craft were trimming and stitching with precision on the most exquisite pieces of fabric she had ever seen. Maybe this sojourn in the palazzo would not be so hard. She could learn from these women who were so clearly masters of their craft.

But then Anna said, "She needs to work in quiet, to concentrate. Give her instructions and I will take her back to her room."

The head embroideress spoke to Carina and then gave her the cloth for her to work on and the beads and thread. Back down the gloomy passageways they walked to her room. Anna watched her and made sure she had all she needed.

Carina was given a free-hand assignment that did not require her loom but would test her capability to follow instructions carefully and with aesthetic prowess. She sat on her bed and opened the little box of beads. They were surely from Murano. Never had she seen such delicate glasswork. Relieved to be with her work, she began the task of beading the collar of a cape and barely registered the sound of the key turning as Anna once again locked the door.

From her window, Carina was privy to the comings and goings in the palazzo courtyard. The sounds of the unfolding day filtered up. She heard Lucrezia's strident tone as she waited for her carriage and the young duchess's voice. She had finished her fitting, and Carina heard her talking to Massimo. She put down her work and moved to the window to observe them. Astride a horse that skittered in the courtyard, Massimo bid goodbye to Donatella. With a clatter of hooves, he and his entourage exited.

Unbeknownst to Carina, Massimo and his footmen made the ride up the Florentine hillside to arrive in Settignano. Massimo's heart lightened at the sight of the Maestro's property, as if he could sense the warmth and love embodied in the stone building with its slanting tile roof. A profusion of flowers spilled over the wall and even the dogs seemed to remember him. His entourage, however, was not pleased to be there, as their priority was to hunt for boar in the countryside. Pietro had forewarned the Maestro of Massimo's visit, and even though the Studio was in its usual activity with his apprentices present and working, the Maestro appeared to greet Massimo and congratulate him on his upcoming marriage.

Pietro's portrait of Donatella was in full view, and Massimo expressed his admiration of Pietro's artistic prowess. His portrait had captured the beauty and liveliness of Donatella. Massimo then toured the Studio, fascinated by the other paintings in progress which were set up on their easels in all corners. The Maestro walked with the young duke, explaining the subject matter of each painting, and when Massimo expressed interest in the technique and the types of material used, the Maestro spoke to him of the paints made from saffron and the rare blue created by crushing lapis lazuli. One of the Maestro's newest paintings of Carina in her flower garden, accompanied by Buono and Buona, caught Massimo's attention. He recognized that the model for this painting was the same young woman in the paintings that he had been admiring in Lucrezia's palazzo the evening before.

Expressing his curiosity, Massimo asked, "Who is she? She looks so familiar."

"That is our Carina," the Maestro offered. "You might remember her and the meals she prepared for her less fortunate friends, thanks to your generosity."

"Of course!" said Massimo. "And I was fortunate enough to attend one a few years ago."

Massimo then asked the Maestro if any of his paintings were available for purchase, as he would very much like to own one.

"The only un-commissioned work of art that I could give you is the recent portrait of Carina."

"Would you be willing to part with it?" Massimo asked.

"I will give it to you in response to you and your family's generosity to her in the past, which we all have appreciated tremendously."

The Maestro called for Pietro and instructed him to include the small portrait of Carina when Pietro delivered his portrait of Donatella to the palazzo. After a brief puzzled glance at Massimo, Pietro said he would do so. Massimo accepted the Maestro's gracious gift and expressed his hope to see him again soon. He and his entourage then made their way into the countryside.

A whirlwind of activity in the palazzo filled the week, in striking contrast with Carina's lonely hours of isolation in her chamber while she embroidered the assigned projects on her loom. As her needle pierced her jewel-encrusted canvas, it expressed the piercing aches of Carina's heart, as if inflicting pain.

Periodically, Anna took Carina to Donatella's fittings in the wardrobe workroom. During these fittings, Carina's heart felt wrenched as Donatella modeled her party dresses and wedding gown, resplendent with Carina's bejeweled handiwork. The older seamstresses and embroideress greatly admired Carina's accomplished embroidery beadwork, and it encouraged her that they appreciated having her as a collaborator.

The workroom was always buzzing with gossip about Donatella's petulant complaints, and Carina overheard the seamstresses hinting that Donatella and the young Duke were not in harmony, although it certainly would not deter their marriage. When Donatella and Anna were not present, the head seamstress suggested a reason for Donatella's unenthusiastic response to her husband to be. "Duke Massimo is always focusing on his athletic training, rather than spending his time fawning over Duchess Donatella, and that seems to irritate her. It appears that his priority is to prepare for his performance carrying the Sienese banner at the upcoming Palio horse race competition in Siena rather than his upcoming marriage to Donatella!"

Carina had heard about the Palio horse race of Siena but had never witnessed it. Lydia and the Maestro always had concerns for her safety in the raucous crowd that gathered to watch noblemen and commoners race lap after lap around Siena's beautiful scallop-shaped piazza. The Palio was a yearly egalitarian affair, one of the few times when the common folk had an opportunity to challenge those more noble than they on common ground. Pietro went every year and had often returned with stories about the Palio: how each neighborhood had its own banner and chose its strongest rider to wear its colors to compete, how the citizens of Siena cleared out the piazza and packed down dirt mixed with hay over the cobblestones, creating a track upon which the horses could race. Each neighborhood strived to best outfit their horse, rider and banner with their striking designs and colors displayed during the race.

Now that she was able to spend time out of the brace and her posture and strength had improved so dramatically, the thought that she might actually see the Palio brightened the day for Carina, especially when she saw how excitedly the other seamstresses chatted about it. Hopefully Lydia and the Maestro would let her go and watch Duke Massimo representing his noble neighborhood in the race. But she soon dismissed the idea with a frown. Massimo was betrothed to

Donatella, and Carina needed to put all thoughts of him out of her head. And as if to confirm the gloom that descended on her, Anna returned to the seamstresses' room to survey the work and then scurried Carina back to her miserable quarters.

The work on the trousseau was coming along nicely, but Anna felt increasingly agitated. She had been having dreams about the babe she had abandoned in the piazza, waking up in a sweat, her breath shallow. She knew what she had to do. She spent hours convincing herself that it was for the best, that it would be fast and painless; she would be sure of it. And still, there were moments when she was suddenly close to tears as she remembered the infant's beautiful features, the features of the girl who would make sure Donatella's wedding dress would be talked about for years to come.

Anna had a close call one day when Lydia arrived unexpectedly at the palazzo. One of the servants was about to take her up to Carina's room when Anna intercepted her. The Maestro's servant woman was agitated, as apparently the Maestro had fallen ill. She wanted to tell Carina and also offer her encouragement, as she knew Carina must be working hard.

"Wait just a few more days. Carina is happy and working well and we are all so impressed with the quality of her embroidery," Anna told her. "When she is finished, she can return to the Studio." With that Anna dismissed Lydia and nodded to a court servant to show her back down the stairs and out of the palazzo.

With the wedding just weeks away the palazzo was abuzz with preparation for the festivities. Lucrezia roamed the halls and bothered the servants with never-ending instructions for the wedding dinner. Donatella alternated between delight in the garments being made for her and periods of gloom when she contemplated being married to Massimo. He rode daily since arriving in Florence, recognizing that this was an opportunity for him to interact with the young Florentine noblemen and establish tactful diplomatic relationships with them. They, in turn, were delighted to race with the young Duke. Each morning Carina heard the clatter of horses' hooves as he left to train, and once again her heart ached, and each evening she strummed her dulcimer, the sweet sounds giving her comfort.

Across the hills and up in his Studio in Settignano, the Maestro continued to decline into the incapacitating illness of old age. Lydia did her best to take care of him, and Pietro painstakingly put the polishing touches on his portrait of Donatella, regretting the day he would have to let loose of it.

Chapter Twenty

Early the following Sunday, Anna made her way to the kitchen, where she gave the cook instructions to prepare an elaborate breakfast for Carina. Seeing the resistance from the cook, who thought it highly unusual to be making a special tray for someone who simply worked in the palazzo, Anna said, "The girl has been working hard, and everyone will be talking about Donatella's wardrobe. I want to reward her."

The cook set a dish of egg soufflé on the tray and a cup of black coffee.

"Give her cream," Anna insisted.

The cook cast Anna a sideways glance but did as she was instructed.

"And some of the berry compote," Anna said, pointing to a mouthwatering pot of compote that was surely intended to be set on the breakfast table for Duchess Lucrezia and her family and noble guests.

The cook gave her another glance, but again she complied. Anna was Lucrezia's foremost long-standing confidante, and everyone wanted to keep in her good graces.

With the tray attractively arranged, Anna cast her eye around the kitchen. Ah, that would be the appropriate final delicious treat, she thought, and she walked to the table where the palazzo bakers had set out freshly baked panettone, Torta della Nonna and Schiaciata all'Uva. Anna chose an individual sized, magnificently baked panettone pastry, resplendent with spun currant jelly and powdered sugar, and set it on the tray.

With a curt nod to the cook, Anna carried the tray down the long corridors and up the stairs to her own bedchamber, where she shut the door and locked it. She set the tray down on her bed, the very bed where Carina had lain so helplessly as a newborn. She searched out a vial of white powder and dusted the beautiful panettone with its contents. What else could she do? She had thought she'd been compassionate when she left the babe in the piazza of Settignano, but no, she'd been weak. If she had followed through on Lucrezia's wishes — and who was she to go against her mistress? — she would not be in this predicament. She had no choice but to use the slow acting poison. She slipped the empty vial into her pocket and headed to Carina's room.

The bird song from the trees in the courtyard ushered in the day Carina had been anticipating. Finally, she would break away from the palazzo and return to Settignano and the Studio for a day of relaxation with her friends. When Anna entered, the smile on Carina's face did nothing to soften her, instead, it only made Anna more resolved. She placed the breakfast tray on the small table, and she wished Carina a good day at the Maestro's Studio. "And I'll see you tonight when you return. Your work on the Duchess Donatella's wardrobe is complete. We'd just like you to be here in case there are any last-minute needs."

Anna left the room, leaving it unlocked for the first time since Carina had arrived at the palazzo some weeks prior.

Alone in her room, Carina looked appreciatively at her breakfast tray. She practically gobbled the eggs. She spooned the fragrant compote into her mouth slowly, savoring it.

Finally, she reached for the added treat of the panettone and held it up before her to examine its delicious beauty. The spun sugar glistened temptingly.

But instead of eating it, Carina set the panettone down with resolve and wrapped it in one of her large handkerchiefs. It would be a gift for the Maestro. She had just slipped it in her small, embroidered travelling satchel when Anna entered the room again, announcing that Pietro was waiting for her. Anna scooped up the empty breakfast tray. "Good, I'm glad you enjoyed it. Well-deserved for a young woman who has worked so hard on the Duchess Donatella's wardrobe. Come," she said.

In Carina's haste to leave the palazzo she had not taken the time to put on her back brace, and left it dangling on the wall, thinking that it might be necessary for her to use when she returned. In fact, she was proud that she would be returning to the Studio without it, as if it were a good report regarding her physical condition. She wanted, as best she could, to hide from the Maestro the miserable time she'd had in the palazzo, and planned to make light of the long hours, the skimpy meals and the inexplicable confinement and isolation she had been enduring. But she knew she would share these things with Lydia, her confidante, because the treatment was so puzzling.

Pietro was waiting for Carina in the courtyard, and Samuele assisted her as she clambered up into the cart, and they set off for Settignano. There was surely not a lovelier morning, and she was going to see her beloved Maestro and Lydia. But Pietro had bad news for her. As they twisted their way up the hills toward the Studio, he revealed that the Maestro had fallen gravely ill during the week and was bedridden. Carina queried Pietro as to what was the cause of the Maestro's poor condition, but he could not respond other than to say that the Maestro was very aged. Carina felt despondent, and even the glimpses of the Duomo set off against the bluest sky, visible at the higher switchbacks on the road, did nothing to lighten her mood.

Carina had wanted to stop at the baker in Settignano on the way to the Studio so as to purchase some bread to augment the Sunday afternoon meal for the outcasts. However, Pietro told her that the gravity of the Maestro's illness was so great that it behooved them to return hastily to the Studio and worry about her beggars' banquet later. They arrived at the Studio where the crunching sound of wheels and the horse's hooves on the gravel entranceway attracted the attention of the dogs, who raced out to meet them, yelping with joy at seeing their best friend, Carina. Buono and Buona circled the cart, jumping up and down as Carina greeted them, reaching out to embrace the dogs as she awkwardly descended. With her feet on the ground, Carina steadied herself and reached back into the cart to retrieve her satchel with her precious panettone for the Maestro. In the excitement of the moment, the dogs caught a whiff of the delicious pastry, and they lunged at the satchel, thinking that surely Carina had brought something special for them! Carina tried to hold the satchel with the panettone over her head, but she lost her balance and began to keel over, dropping it all to the ground and gripping onto the cart with both hands to steady herself. The dogs grabbed the satchel, playfully dragging it out of reach from Carina. "No!" she cried. Samuel chased after the dogs as they ran, snatching the satchel back and forth, dragging it through a muddy puddle from the previous night's rain.

At this moment Lydia emerged from the Studio to greet Carina and chided Buona and Buono over the ruckus they were making, which was inappropriate considering the need for quiet for the ailing Maestro. Lydia grabbed Carina's satchel with the now ruined panettone from the dogs, and holding it at an arm's distance, she embraced and warmly greeted Carina and ushered her inside.

There was an eerie hush over the Studio. Lydia had been preparing a welcome lunch for Carina, but there was no evidence of a full-blown beggars' banquet.

"Let me look at you, Carina. How have they been treating my girl?" Lydia queried.

Carina responded, "Don't worry about me. How is the Maestro?"

"Bad, bad. And all your friends know about it, so I cancelled today's usual festivities."

Carina's voice trembled with emotion as she spoke. "They're not coming? I missed everyone so much."

Lydia had been standing at the stove, preparing coffee for herself and Carina. She paused to examine Carina carefully, assessing her pale pallor. "Are you all right?"

Ignoring Lydia's question, Carina said, "I wanted to bring all of you gifts from the palazzo, but the pickings were meager. And the one panettone I saved was ruined by the dogs!"

"Don't worry, love. It's your presence that matters."

"Tell me about Maestro. I want to see him."

Lydia sat down with Carina at the kitchen table. "He's just plain sick with old age. Wait a bit and talk to me. Pietro's with him right now. Tell me about your time at the palazzo."

"I can't understand it," Carina said, shaking her head. "I worked hard, but they isolated me from the other seamstresses and made me do the embroidery alone in my room. But they were very pleased with my work!"

"Oh, you're probably just thrown off balance because you're away from us and it's all new. And I see you are not wearing your brace. That's good!"

"I was in such a hurry to leave and return home that I forgot to put it on. I feel good, fairly strong. But I expected to find a more generous welcome at the palazzo. It is so strange."

Trying to encourage Carina, Lydia put her arm around her gently. "You just steel yourself like flint and do good work. Keep praying unto the Lord, and He will strengthen and guide you. You are so gifted, and I am glad to hear they appreciate your skills."

At this moment Pietro came into the kitchen, having been with the Maestro. "Lydia, come. The Maestro wants to speak to you."

Carina offered, "I can fix his breakfast tray."

"You do that. But he's not very enthusiastic about food right now," Lydia said, as she and Pietro returned to the Maestro's bedroom.

The panettone that Carina had hoped to serve the Maestro was indeed ruined, but she could still pick some flowers for the Maestro's breakfast tray, so she exited and was greeted, once again, by the dogs who had missed her loving caresses. She chose blue cornflowers and delicate anemones.

The Maestro lay propped up on bed pillows, eyes closed, and breathing with some difficulty. Pietro and Lydia stood quietly beside him. Discerning their presence, the Maestro opened his eyes and began speaking to them. "It won't be long now, and I want you to know how the Studio must be carried on. Pietro, with God's good grace, you will be in charge of the Studio and become the Maestro, creating masterpieces and sharing your talent with other aspiring artists. Pietro, you have an artistic gift that will carry you wherever you want and will always guarantee you an income. Lydia has been so loyal, and I want to ensure her security. Therefore, although you are guaranteed the use of and headship over the work in the Studio for your lifetime, the building will be bequeathed to Lydia. Therefore, she can feel safe and secure knowing that she will never be ousted, and she will also be careful to protect my vulnerable little Carina. Where is she? Where is Carina?"

Lydia kissed the Maestro's hand in thanks to him, and left to fetch Carina for the Maestro, who sank back into his pillows with closed eyes. Pietro, now alone with the Maestro, contemplated this surprising change of plans for the Studio's future. Pietro had hoped to be in full control, but acknowledging the Maestro's extraordinary compassion and generosity, he knew he had to accept the Maestro's decision to protect Lydia and Carina's futures.

Happy to at last be home in her kitchen, Carina put the flowers she had picked in a small vase and set them on the Maestro's breakfast tray and then proceeded through the Studio to the Maestro's room. Appearing at first to be asleep when she entered, the Maestro revived and greeted her. Carina placed the breakfast tray at his bedside and perched herself next to him. He queried her about her experience at the palazzo. They quietly conversed, though it was difficult for the Maestro, both relishing the deep intimacy they had built up over the years.

Already weak, the Maestro's concentration began to wane, and Carina encouraged him to rest. As he closed his eyes and sank back further into his pillows, Carina took his hand, talking quietly to him. "My dear, beloved Maestro, you have been a loving light for me along with dearest Lydia. I am eternally grateful unto the Lord for your care and devotion." The Maestro's love had been until now the fulfillment of Carina's needs, but Carina discerned with alarm that the Maestro would not be with them much longer, and for the first time she spoke out loud her desires. "Oh, my dear Maestro, I pray that I can have a love of my own one day, as I am sure that is your desire for me also."

Carina was not prepared to see the Maestro so weakened, and in a daze she went into the Studio and seated herself on the pedestal where for so many years she had posed for him. Looming in front of her was his last portrait of her. How could she be that gracious and serene lady facing her on the canvas? The Maestro had been the person who most appreciated Carina's beauty, her inner beauty. She felt his love emanating from his careful brush strokes. She glanced over to some of her embroidered tapestries on a wall. She would not have been able to develop her beadwork embroidery skills without the help and encouragement of the Maestro. What would life be like without him? She wept.

Pietro entered the Studio, and after a moment of silence he approached Carina and embraced her. They had grown up in the Studio, both benefactors of the Maestro. Then he told her it was time to return to the palazzo, and Lydia wanted her to have something to eat before she returned. While

Lydia and Carina had a hasty lunch together, Pietro carefully wrapped his portrait of Donatella, and also the small portrait of Carina that the Maestro had instructed him to deliver to Duke Massimo. Then they set off in the cart and slowly made their way back to Florence.

Chapter Twenty-One

Anna approached the delivery entrance of the palazzo with a sense of resolve. The messenger had announced that Pietro had arrived with the portrait just in time for the unveiling that evening.

"Did he say anything else?" she asked the messenger.

"Yes, the Maestro is failing. All of Settignano is concerned."

"Since when?" Anna demanded.

But the messenger had no answer.

"The girl, the one who does the embroidery, did he say anything about her?"

"No, she is just waiting by the cart."

"What? Out, out of my way!" Anna cried, as she hurried into the courtyard. She felt shaken. Was the Maestro's weakness somehow connected with her own wickedness?

Having been deposited by Samuele at the side entrance, Carina felt abandoned. She knew that she was expected to maintain her contractual commitment to be available to complete last-minute details on Donatella's wedding gown. Tears welled up in her as she stood contemplating her situation there. Where did she belong?

As Carina stood vacillating, she saw a figure hurrying toward her. It was Anna. She looked at Carina with a stricken expression, and Carina felt compassion for this woman. She'd never trusted her, never felt truly comfortable in her presence, but Anna's pale face softened Carina's feelings, and she vowed to make the most of her remaining time in the palazzo. She would do her best work; it was what she owed the Maestro, in gratitude for the opportunities he had given her.

"The Maestro is ill? What happened?" Anna asked.

"I don't know. Lydia said he is very old."

Once again Carina followed Anna up and down staircases and through the corridors of the servants' quarters. By the time they reached her room it seemed that the old Anna had returned, abrupt and demanding, a smile never crossing her face, a kind word never being spoken. Disregarding Carina's exhausted condition, Anna demanded Carina sew a few stitches before retiring, promising to bring her dinner. And again, Anna locked Carina in her room.

Meanwhile, at the far end of the palazzo in one of the bedrooms of the lavish guest quarters, Massimo meditated on the small portrait, the Maestro's gift to him that Pietro had just delivered. A heavy stillness pervaded the room while shafts of light crossed the mantelpiece, illuminating Carina's composed visage. Massimo barely registered the presence of his valet who entered and lit the candles on the mantel, and quietly said, "It's time, sir."

When Massimo made no sign of having heard him the valet cleared his throat. "Sir?"

With a weary sigh Massimo moved away from the Maestro's painting and held out one arm and then the other as the valet helped him into his vestments for the evening. On the morrow he and his family would be returning to Siena so that he could race in the Palio the following day. The thought of racing around the Piazza Del Campo gave him more pleasure than the evening's upcoming festivities.

The sounds of music and laughter filtering up to her small room in the servants' quarters was salt in the wound and added to the deep sadness Carina felt. She slumped on the bed, questioning all the work she had done, the years in the brace, the strenuous exercises, the encouragement from the Maestro, Lydia, Sister Clara. What would her life be like when her beloved Maestro finally departed? The scriptures she had memorized of Jesus's words and God's promises began to flow into her heart and mind; "Peace I leave with you; my peace I give you. I do not give to you as the world gives. Do not let your heart be troubled and do not be afraid." Although Carina felt disheartened, she cleaved to her faith and believed that, as He promised, God would lead, guide, and provide for her.

She was still curled in her bed, praying, when Anna entered an hour later with a dinner tray.

Seeing Carina lying in bed, Anna demanded "Why aren't you working? Are you sick?"

When Carina didn't respond Anna continued, "Ah, I know, you ate too much of the panettone I served you. I saw you ate it all!"

"No. I am not sick. I took the panettone up to the Studio so as to have something special to give to the Maestro. But the dogs destroyed it. The Maestro is so weak, and I am deeply concerned. I can't eat."

Anna, wide-eyed, put the tray on the table beside Carina's bed. She stood by Carina who lay quietly with her eyes closed.

Overwhelmed at how her plan had failed and dreading what Lucrezia would do if she knew of her actions, Anna's whole life passed before her eyes. She began to tremble. Anna left the uneaten dinner tray behind and exited.

While Carina lay curled up on her bed, the dinner honoring Donatella and Massimo proceeded. With the climactic build-up toward the presentation of Pietro's portrait of Donatella — considering all the attention paid to her costume and the details of the dinner — everyone was disappointed with Massimo's polite but unenthusiastic reception. The only compliments came from the other guests, and although those present lauded the portrait's beauty, Massimo's lack of appreciation irked Donatella. In fact, she noticed that Massimo seemed to have more eyes for the Maestro's "Baptism of Christ" which hung on the wall in the dining chamber than for his wedding portrait. She commented, rather rudely, that perhaps he had more of a bent for the priesthood than for marriage, considering the subject of that painting.

The conversation at dinner centered less upon Donatella and more upon the upcoming Palio horse race. Donatella unleashed her frustrations with some high-stepping dancing, but despite the spirited music, there was an uncomfortable pall over the occasion. Massimo excused himself early and retired for the night, citing the need for rest in anticipation of the Palio. Donatella was gracious as she watched him go, but Anna, who knew the young duchess well, noticed a look of quiet fury cross her face. After a few minutes Donatella too excused herself. When Anna rose to follow her, she glared at her and shook her head. Anna stopped. What did it matter? With Carina still in the room upstairs, she had more problems to deal with than that of a spoiled and impetuous duchess.

Chapter Twenty-Two

*U*pstairs in her bedroom Donatella cried. She threw her hairbrush against the wall and slapped the hand of her maidservant who had come to prepare her for bed. "Leave me alone!"

Like Carina, she too curled up in her bed. She stared moodily at the ceiling for a while, thinking that the gloomy atmosphere of the evening was surely so because of Massimo's anticipation of competing in the Palio. She smiled, however, thinking of herself on the royal viewing platform, watching the horses fly by, and then bedecked in the finest gown as she wed her groom, who would surely win the race. He had been practicing and practicing. She frowned momentarily. Had his training for the Palio received more attention than she? Her grandmother had assured her that arranged marriages often blossomed into marriages of mutual compatibility. But Donatella wanted more than that. The moon had risen and its soft light shone through her window. It was a night for lovers, and it wasn't too late. Determined to bring some spark to her upcoming marriage, Donatella sat up with a sly expression. She donned a robe, brushed her hair, then carefully opened her bedroom door. There was not a soul in sight.

She tiptoed down passageways and into the apartment antechamber outside Massimo's bedroom. She looked around to orient herself, not wanting to awaken his valet asleep in an adjacent room, but then she saw the door to Massimo's bedroom. With a smile she opened it and tiptoed toward Massimo, asleep in his bed. She daintily picked up a corner of the bed covers and slipped under them, intending to surprise him with some forbidden kisses. When he did not stir, she inched closer, trying to discern where his sleeping head was hidden. Unable to see under the covers, she blindly placed delicate kisses on him. As Donatella increased the lusciousness of her kisses, Massimo jerked awake, unintentionally thumping Donatella on the chin. The covers flew back, revealing a very surprised Massimo. Donatella leaned against the headboard and rubbed her sore jaw as Massimo sat up and faced her.

"What . . . why . . . why are you here?" he said in alarm.

"I wanted to give you a few goodnight kisses before you left for the Palio," she said. A flush rose to her cheek and she moved closer to him. "For good luck," she added. "Of course, I'll be there to cheer you on—" Donatella stopped in mid-sentence and stared at the small portrait displayed on the mantel. Massimo followed her gaze, and for an instant they both focused on Carina's beautiful countenance. Momentarily confused, Donatella looked dumbly from the portrait to her betrothed and back to the portrait. "What is that?"

And to her dismay Massimo responded in a gentle tone. "It is one of the Maestro's portraits. He gifted it to me."

Donatella hunched her shoulders and jumped off the bed. She stamped her foot and hissed, "Do you know who she is?"

"She is one of the Maestro's models whom he has had living at the Studio ever since he found her abandoned in the piazza of Settignano."

"She's nothing but a mere seamstress working on my wedding gown! An embroideress! And a misfit!"

"She's here in the palazzo?" There was no denying the flash of light that came into Massimo's eyes when he asked this.

"Why should she interest you? She doesn't exist as far as you're concerned!" said Donatella, and she stalked out, her head reared high.

Shortly before dawn the clatter of hooves in the courtyard once again roused Carina. She had barely slept, and now she moved to the window hoping to see Massimo. It would surely be the last time — and that was best, she told herself. But her heart still ached as she watched him mount his horse. She knew from talk in the palazzo that he would be in Siena to prepare for the Palio. Would that she could be leaving along with Duke Massimo! She longed to be set free from her imprisoned chamber. Carina spoke out, "Oh Lord, deliver me."

A sudden pounding on the door startled her. She heard a shrill, angry voice proclaiming, "I'll tear off every single bead and jewel she embroidered onto my clothes! She'll never sew another stitch as long as she lives!"

Carina then heard someone frantically attempting to turn the key in the lock. Fearing that her work on the wedding trousseau had been shoddy, Carina moved to the corner of the room and waited for her punishment.

The door flew open. Carina briefly saw Anna standing there in her nightgown, and then she was pushed aside as the furious young Duchess Donatella stormed into the middle of the room. The accusations came fast and furious. How dare she, a mere commoner, a no-good seamstress, try to break up her engagement to Massimo! She needed to leave the palazzo immediately!

Carina stood their stunned, barely able to absorb the accusations, and then to her horror Duchess Lucrezia appeared in the doorway, she too in her nightclothes, pleading for an explanation to quickly end this disturbance.

"Explanation? Explain this!" cried Donatella. She stomped out of Carina's bedroom, Lucrezia and Anna following behind, shaking their un-coiffed heads while their sleeping wraps fluttered feverishly.

The confrontation with Donatella, the departure of Massimo, the knowledge that the Maestro was failing — it was all too much for Carina, and she wanted nothing more than to leave the palazzo. With the accusations still ringing in her ears, she slipped out in search of a refuge, a place where she could grieve and cry.

Anna had never seen Donatella so agitated, and she had witnessed most of the young Duchess's temper tantrums. The accusations Donatella had hurled at Carina were outlandish. But slowly it made sense to her when they caught up with Donatella in Massimo's bedroom. Hands on hips, Donatella faced the portrait of Carina over the mantel. "What is SHE doing up there?" she asked bitterly. Turning to face her uncharacteristically disheveled grandmother, Donatella cried, "I want to know!"

Anna stared in horror at the portrait.

Lucrezia turned to Anna and then Donatella and then back to Anna. "Can someone please tell me—" But Lucrezia couldn't finish her sentence because Donatella burst into tears. She swept past her grandmother and practically knocked over her uncle, Duke Onorio, in the hallway. He had become aware of the noise in Massimo's quarters and entered the antechamber, unnoticed by Lucrezia and Anna who remained in Massimo's bedroom, staring at the portrait of Carina.

Regaining her composure, Lucrezia addressed Anna. "Who is that?"

"It's her! It's her. She has come back to haunt us," Anna babbled.

Lucrezia stepped closer — after all, it was a small work. "Is that the seamstress from the Maestro's Studio?" She narrowed her eyes to focus on the portrait. "I never noticed before . . . but does she not resemble—"

Before Lucrezia could say another word, Anna remembered that Carina had been left alone in her room and she too raced out, whipping past Duke Onorio in the antechamber, with Lucrezia fast on her heels. Now it was the Duke's turn to move closer to the portrait. The young woman had a beauty about her, a pensive expression that reminded him of his late wife, his beloved Grazia. Intensely curious, he left the apartment and followed the sounds of the agitated voices of his mother and her maidservant, echoing down the long hallways of the palazzo as they rushed back to the servants' quarters.

He arrived at Carina's room in time to overhear Lucrezia demand once again, "Who is she? Why are you so concerned about the seamstress?"

The room was empty except for Carina's few belongings and her abandoned back brace hanging on the wall over her bed. Lucrezia saw the brace and looked at it with a strange expression, this being the first time she knew anything of Carina's physical deformity. "What is that? What is that thing? Does that belong to her?"

As Anna stared numbly at the back brace, she imagined herself strapped into it, dangling helplessly, pinned up on the wall, her legs and arms flailing like an insect with its belly vulnerably exposed, unable to escape. She had no recourse, and she numbly spoke the truth. "It's the babe. You thought she was dead. But she's come back to life."

Lucrezia began to grasp the meaning of this, and she gripped Anna by the shoulder. "You mean . . . how can it be? How do you know?" she whispered.

The Duke did not yet comprehend the meaning of this conversation, but, unobserved, he drew closer to the women, watching and listening intently.

"Carina is not the Maestro's daughter," Anna said, relieving herself of the burden she had carried for so many years. "He and his assistant found her in the piazza of Settignano where I abandoned the babe 18 years ago, and they raised her. She is Duke Onorio and Duchess Grazia's daughter."

At first, Lucrezia was too shocked to react to this appalling confession, her mind awhirl with memories of Grazia's cries, and the misshapen form of the child. Seeking privacy, she moved to close the door, only to bump into her eldest son who stood there with a look of astonishment.

Lucrezia pleaded for the first time in her life. "I didn't know. After your beloved Grazia died I thought the babe had also died. Please, believe me."

"Where is she?" Duke Onorio demanded.

Lucrezia could barely muster the words to say, "I don't know."

Duke Onorio took command of the situation now, understanding fully the meaning of the conversation. For the moment, he did not confront his mother and her servant with their dastardly lie. Seeing only the possibility that his dead daughter was resurrected, the Duke immediately went to the guards at the entrance of the palazzo to ask if they had seen Carina exit. When they answered "Yes," he had them saddle up his horse, and accompanied by two servants, he rode to the Maestro's Studio in Settignano hoping to find Carina there.

Chapter Twenty-Three

The Florentines were busy with their early morning activities, while Carina walked aimlessly up one cobblestone street and down the other. She felt as if she had failed her beloved Maestro and Lydia. Her steps drew her towards the Duomo cathedral where she heard bells tolling in their call for the first morning mass. The gleaming Duomo cupola come into view, and she stopped and looked up, speaking out loud again, "Please God, help me!"

Carina entered the cathedral as she had many times in the past with the Maestro and Lydia to attend mass. Afterwards she would always pay a visit to Adamo. She decided to do so now. He had been such a good friend to her, her only friend in the city of Florence. As Carina began to mount the bell tower steps, Adamo was descending. He was surprised to see Carina and was concerned by her sorrowful expression. He wished he could stay and talk to her, but he explained, "My family is leaving right away to go to Siena for the Palio. I must help them." Carina remembered that Adamo's mother was Sienese, and every year they would go to Siena to cheer on the riders from her quartiere as they raced. They also sold their baked goods to the throng gathered for the race.

Carina was torn for a moment, but she gathered her courage and dared to ask Adamo if she could come with them. Remembering Carina's loyal generosity to him, he did not hesitate. "Certainly you can join us. But we are leaving right away!"

Carina did not want to leave Florence without Lydia and the Maestro knowing. "I want to come, but I need to send word somehow to the Studio!"

"We can ask one of the bakery workers to go up to Settignano to let the Maestro know, as my family will be waiting and ready to leave," said Adamo.

And so, Carina and Adamo headed to the bakery, Carina assisting Adamo with his belabored walking, as his deformity continued to hinder him. On arrival at the bakery, Adamo instructed one of the workers to go to the Studio to give the Maestro Carina's message. It would have to wait for a few hours, the worker told them, as they still had to finish baking the bread they sold daily to the Florentines.

Adamo, his parents and Carina piled into the cart and started their journey to Siena, surrounded with the many baskets of bread and pastries. Adamo's father insisted Carina partake of some of the goods, as she had not eaten breakfast. Adamo was pleased to see the tables turned; after so many years of being a guest at the beggars' banquet it was now his turn to nourish Carina with his family's finest pastries and to give her the opportunity to enjoy an outing of fellowship.

As they crossed the Arno and headed south to Siena, Carina pondered her hasty decision to go to the Palio. Being honest with herself, she admitted she was going because she wanted to see Massimo again and witness him competing in the race. But what would it accomplish?

Duke Onorio rode at a fast pace, and by the time he reached the Maestro's Studio in Settignano, the fury he felt at the lies and deceit about his daughter's death had been replaced with a tender hope that he could find her. He banged on the door and Pietro answered it. Stepping inside,

Duke Onorio recalled that the Maestro was gravely ill, and he spoke quietly and inquired about his condition. He then asked Pietro if Carina was at the Studio.

"No, she left for the palazzo after visiting with the Maestro yesterday."

Duke Onorio paused. He felt nervous to ask the next question. Could it really be that his daughter was alive? "I want to know about her parentage. Can you tell me something of how she came to stay with the Maestro, as I understand she is not his daughter by birth."

Pietro told the story of how he and the Maestro had found the babe in the piazza of Settignano, having witnessed her abandonment by a horse and rider. "She was deformed, but in time, with the help of Doctor Benedetto, Carina gained strength and was able to overcome her deformities."

"And she was found on what day?"

"She was found on May 22nd, the day before my 10th birthday."

With this confirmation, tears came to the Duke's eyes, and he grasped Pietro's hands. "Thank you. Thank you. She is my daughter, the one I thought I lost so many years ago."

"Carina?" Pietro said, as stunned as Duke Onorio. "She is your daughter? A duchess?"

"But where is she?" Duke Onorio asked again. "Do you know where she might go?"

"She should be at the palazzo. Is she not there?"

"No. She left on her own several hours ago," Duke Onorio said, not wanting to speak about the confrontation with Donatella. "I am going to return to the palazzo now, but I must leave for Siena as planned so as to be present at the Palio with the Sienese ducal family. Please, if there is any way you can search for her, I will be immensely grateful. I and my family will be guests in the palazzo in Siena, so you can find me there if you need me."

Pietro assured Duke Onorio that he would do his best to find her.

Duke Onorio hastily returned to the palazzo to speak to his younger brother Eduardo about this astonishing news and to talk to his mother. Duke Eduardo was stupefied at first, but he then expressed his joy to his brother. It had pained him so long to witness his brother's grief. "To have a daughter return from the dead is a blessing," he shared. He then advised Onorio to talk to their mother after the Palio.

Within the hour the horses were harnessed and the carriage ready to depart. The Florentine ducal family crossed over the Arno, and they too made their way to Siena. Duke Onorio felt deeply perturbed; Carina was still missing, and he uneasily pondered the future in the uncomfortable presence of his royal relatives. Duke Eduardo and Duchess Francesca accompanied him with Donatella.

"Where is La Nonna?" Donatella asked.

Duke Onorio explained that Lucrezia was not feeling well and remained behind.

"Oh, I hope I did not upset her because I found that portrait of that Carina girl in Massimo's bedroom! It certainly upset me!" she cried out. "And Anna? Is she not coming?"

Duchess Francesca responded to her daughter. "Anna stayed with Lucrezia. We will talk about it all when we get to Siena." Seeing that Donatella was shaking with tension, her mother put her arm around her and drew Donatella close to her, cuddling her, hoping to console her.

But Duke Onorio and his family's level of anxiety did not nearly match that of Duchess Lucrezia and Anna, who were separately sequestered in their quarters at the palazzo, awaiting their earthly judgments.

Before setting off on his search for Carina, Pietro shared with Lydia all that Duke Onorio had revealed about Carina. Lydia was so astonished by this news that she had to pause, steadying herself and then sitting down at the kitchen table. "Our Carina, a duchess? And such a beautiful one at that. I must tell the Maestro."

She rose to her feet, but Pietro stopped her. "She's not at the palazzo and Duke Onorio has entrusted me with searching for her."

While the two of them thought of all the places that she might be, there was a knock on the kitchen door. The baker from Adamo's family bakery had arrived with the news that Carina had gone to Siena with Adamo and his family.

When questioned as to where they would stay in Siena, the baker did not know. "But Adamo and his family will be selling our baked goods the morning of the Palio at the main cathedral, where there will be the blessing of the horses and riders. Carina will surely be there also."

Pietro had not planned to go to the Palio due to the Maestro's weak condition, but now he immediately saddled his horse and joined the other travelers on the road to Siena.

Alone in the kitchen, Lydia once again marveled at the news. Her girl —because that was how she thought of the babe she had looked after, who had grown into such a beautiful young woman, modest and kind and generous — was now a member of the ducal family. Would she be living in the palazzo? She patted Buona and Buono who had entered the kitchen, always on the hunt for scraps. "You two will have to stay here with me. I can't see you at the palazzo, and I need your company."

Lydia rose, pensive, and made her way to the Maestro's quarters at the far end of the Studio. She gently opened the door to his room but found he was sleeping. He looked so frail, weakened. She hesitated to wake him and sat awhile in the chair by his bedside, filled with gratitude for the Maestro and the choice he made to bring Carina into their home. What a blessing it had been for all of them. He stirred, and his eyes fluttered open briefly.

"Maestro," she whispered, "I have the most wonderful news about our Carina." Sensing that it was not the right moment to go into the details, not just yet, she simply said, "She is well, and she loves you."

Lydia was looking forward to sharing this good news about Carina with the Maestro when he awoke later.

Pietro rode at a brisk pace toward Siena and scanned the crowds on the road. He passed merchants and carriages with families, all going to watch the Palio the following day. He kept a lookout for the baker and his family, but there was no sign of them or Carina. Unbeknownst to him, Adamo's family had stopped, as they did every year, at a relative's home to change horses, leaving their horse to rest until the next day and borrowing a horse to complete their journey. Pietro passed them and arrived in Siena ahead of them. It was already dusk, and as instructed, he made his way to the Sienese ducal palazzo.

This was not the first time Pietro had visited Siena to view the Palio. As he approached the palazzo which directly faced the Piazza del Campo where the race was always conducted, he felt the importance of this visit. A servant admitted him to the Sienese palazzo and escorted him to a receiving room. There he found Duke Onorio sharing the news of Carina's true heritage. The Duke and Duchess of Siena, along with Massimo, Donatella and her parents were all present. Duke Onorio asked Pietro to share his knowledge about Carina and her abandonment in the piazza of Settignano and how Pietro and the Maestro had brought her into the Maestro's home. Pietro reiterated the truth of Carina's history and the reality that Duke Onorio was her father.

"This is wonderful news," said the Duchess of Siena. "I remember her well. We donated our rings so she could raise funds for the meal she prepared for her less fortunate friends. She seemed to be such a tender soul."

Massimo spoke next. "I too remember that, and now she is transformed. It's remarkable! She is the model for many of the Maestro's portraits."

Only Donatella did not offer words of enthusiasm. She looked stunned, and Pietro's heart went out to the young duchess. He knew her to be spoiled, impetuous and also, to his mind, charming. The news must have shocked her, as it did the others, because soon a pause of silence came over them all.

Duke Eduardo broke it and spoke gently to his daughter. "She is your cousin, Donatella. We are so fortunate. And soon we will, God willing, welcome her into our family."

Donatella remained silent. She bit her lip and Pietro saw the tears forming in her eyes.

But he had more to tell them. He shared he had learned that Adamo and his family, and therefore surely Carina, would be selling baked goods in front of the cathedral prior to the service the following morning. The cathedral was adjacent to the ducal palazzo, and Massimo and his horse would be amongst those riders and horses lining up to receive a blessing.

Donatella could not control herself anymore. She cried out, confronting Massimo, "Did you know this? Is that why you had her portrait in your bedroom at our palazzo?"

While Massimo slowly shook his head no, Donatella jumped up and ran out of the room and down into the gardens, where she wept. Duchess Francesca and Pietro hurried after her. Her mother took Donatella in her arms, trying to console her crestfallen daughter. After some time, Pietro approached them and said, "Duchess Donatella, you are a very beautiful, noble lady, and nothing can take that away from you."

Looking at Pietro, Donatella put her hand over her heart, indicating she received and appreciated his kind words.

Chapter Twenty-Four

*M*assimo was the first to rise and face the new day. Full of energy, he looked from the palazzo out over the deserted Piazza del Campo that would soon become the scene of wild, unleashed activity where he would put his physical fortitude to the utmost test. He longed for that, a distraction from the turmoil he felt within as he thought about his impending nuptials.

At the same time as Massimo left for the stable to see the horse he'd been allotted to ride, Adamo, his parents and Carina arrived at the cathedral near the central piazza. The entire city was bedecked with festive decorations of every color, and each edifice surrounding the piazza displayed the banner of a contrada district or a family's coat of arms. Drummers and flag throwers with the colorful banners of their respective neighborhoods soon arrived and circled the piazza. Demonstrating their arts, they intensified the pre-race drama.

Carina helped Adamo and his family set up their bakery stall, and she even assisted with the sales of their goods. Business was brisk, thanks to growing crowds. When most of the pastries were sold, they thanked her and suggested she wait in the cathedral. Carina entered and sat quietly in a pew near the entrance to pray. Her mind was filled with questions and doubt. What was she doing here? What would be her future when she returned to the Studio?

Relatives of those competing and the neighborhood citizens began to come in and seat themselves in the cathedral. Pietro was the first to arrive from the ducal palazzo. He immediately recognized Adamo and his family, and they pointed to Carina inside. When he entered, he seated himself next to Carina and greeted her gently. She was surprised to see him, but it was a comfort to her.

It was not his place to speak of her birthright, and so he said he'd simply come to view the race. He explained that each horse and rider were blessed before the Palio with the rider leading his horse into the chapel or cathedral of their respective contrada. Did she know that this was where Massimo and his horse would receive their blessing? She did not. Just then the Duke and Duchess of Siena arrived, along with Duke Onorio and Donatella and her parents. Normally the ducal families would sit in the front pews of the cathedral, but seeing Pietro with Carina, they seated themselves around her. They quietly greeted her, not wanting to create a stir, but Donatella was silent. Although she remembered the Duke and Duchess of Siena as her previous benefactors at the Maestro's Studio, Carina felt alarmed to be suddenly surrounded by Donatella and her family. She instinctively jumped to her feet and made a move to leave, but Pietro prevented her and carefully pulled her down, whispering into her ear that they were all here to be a blessing to her. Carina gave him a questioning look, uncertain of what he meant by that, and Pietro squeezed her hand in a gesture of confidence. With his other hand he raised his fingers to his lips, indicating that they should quietly wait.

A cheer went up from outside as those from the neighborhood who had not managed to get into the cathedral crowded the steps. Massimo had arrived! Dressed in the colorful attire of blue and white which identified his ducal neighborhood and carrying high the family banner which unfurled its royal identity, he rode his dapple-grey horse bareback to the entrance. Massimo was accompanied by his assistant, and he handed him the family banner and slipped off his horse. A hush fell over the cathedral as Massimo entered and solemnly led his steed down the main aisle. He stopped at the altar where the priest blessed both him and the horse, releasing them with the customary, "Go and return victorious."

Making his way once again back down the aisle between the pews, he was surprised that his family was not seated at the front. He scanned the crowd and saw them towards the rear. As he approached the ducal families, he saw Carina in their midst. Massimo locked eyes with her and smiled, and it struck him that it was so very appropriate to see Carina with them. But there was no time to stop, as he needed to enter the piazza and prepare for the start of the race.

As soon as Massimo left the cathedral, the Duke and Duchess of Siena invited Carina to return with them to their palazzo where they would be viewing the Palio race. The Sienese Duchess saw that Carina was shivering from anxiety, and she took off her shawl and tenderly placed it on Carina's shoulders, wrapping it around her.

When they entered the palazzo, Duke Onorio asked Pietro to bring Carina into a private antechamber. He spoke simply and told her that Duchess Lucrezia and her servant Anna had confessed as to Carina's true origins. Carina could barely comprehend what was being said. She looked desperately at Pietro who reassured her that what was being revealed was true.

How could this be?

Carina's life passed before her eyes as they spoke with her. The God-given provision of the Maestro's and Lydia's care for her touched her heart deeply, along with the realization that the Maestro was close to passing on and would no longer be a protection for her. Duke Onorio was ever so kind as he talked with Carina and tried to alleviate her fears about this life-changing development.

He held her hand, looked into her eyes and said, "Carina, you are my daughter, the daughter I thought I'd lost forever."

Was it possible that the Lord God was now mercifully providing for her future? Carina understood that she had been nourished and had flourished under the Maestro and Lydia's compassionate care, and only now was it God's plan for her life that her rightful heritage be revealed? A surge of forgiveness for Lucrezia and Anna came upon Carina, and she covered her face with her hands. Duke Onorio put his hands reassuringly on her shoulders, and then, for the first time, she smiled at her father.

"I'm not angry with them. I can't be. I thank God for his merciful provision for me. Please, I want them to know," said Carina.

Knowing that the Palio race would soon begin, Duke Onorio, Pietro and Carina left the antechamber to join the other family members on the palazzo's viewing platform.

"Is this true?" she asked herself.

Yes, it is.

Carina's steps grew lighter and lighter as she walked outside. The Duchess of Siena graciously offered Carina a seat between her and Duke Onorio, and she accepted.

Donatella was seated between her parents, but she still felt bewildered by Carina's presence on the platform and all the newly realized developments about her . . . her cousin. Her heart sank because she knew Massimo's feelings for Carina. A chair remained conspicuously empty where Duchess Lucrezia should have been seated.

The noise from the crowd grew boisterous with yells of encouragement and soon became a deafening din. The riders, riding bareback on their horses and dressed in their colorful costumes identifying their neighborhoods, slowly circled the piazza once. As Massimo passed by the platform, the entire family stood up, and Carina was in full view. The way Massimo caressed his horse and spoke gently to him, calming and assuring him before the race began, pulled Carina toward him, for it was Massimo's quiet, calm within, and his tenderness that had endeared and attracted Carina irresistibly to him.

Finally, the time arrived for all horses and their riders to gather at the starting point. The head official's voice was practically drowned out as he stated the rules to the readied horsemen and the number of rounds to be raced around the piazza before a winner was declared. It was by the drop of a lady's handkerchief held high above the crowd that the race always began, along with a gunshot. This year Donatella, although not Sienese, had been given the honor as a token of diplomatic harmony between the cities of Siena and Florence. The horses and riders jockeyed for position, and then with a haughty flick of her wrist, Donatella initiated the race. The gunshot rang out, the handkerchief fluttered to the ground, and horses and riders took off!

The crowd cheered wildly for their neighborhood's horseman. Everyone on the palazzo's viewing platform leapt to their feet, and Carina joined them at the very front edge. In the first round of the race Massimo was in second place, but as he passed by the platform, he could not refrain from looking up to search for Carina, and he slipped to 4th place. Massimo well knew that the Palio race only lasted for three laps, so he steeled himself and urged on his horse with every ounce of energy he could muster. He regained his position of second place in the second round. Determined to win, Massimo launched into the third round and made the risky choice of trying to nose out the front runner from the rail. The whole race only took about 90 seconds, so Massimo's instincts needed to be his very best. And indeed, as they all approached the finish line, Massimo's horse came in one head ahead of the second-place rider.

He had won!

What joy!

Both noble families embraced one another enthusiastically, including Carina as one of them.

A beaming Massimo, still astride his horse, entered the winner's circle, led by the Palio's head official. Breathing heavily, his horse tossed his head triumphantly, his sweat-stained flanks a testament to how he had exerted his utmost strength along with Massimo. Simultaneously, the Duke and Duchess of Siena and the whole family entourage excitedly descended the platform to come to the winner's circle. Duke Onorio took Carina's arm to make sure she arrived safely.

It was the noble family's honor to place a horseshoe-shaped wreath of red roses around the winner's horse's neck, and so the Duke and Duchess of Siena adorned Massimo's steed. It was also a tradition that the winning rider would pick a rose from the wreath and hand it to his favorite lady. Carina was nearest to him and within Massimo's reach, and smiling, he extended his arm to hand the winner's rose to her. At first her breath was taken away, as she knew his gesture gave a clear message. But taking a deep breath and returning his smile, Carina accepted and received his rose, hoping it would fully blossom into a fulfilling relationship.

When you give a banquet, invite the poor, the crippled, the lame, the blind, and you will be blessed.

—Luke 14:13

Acknowledgments

Deep heartfelt thanks to my husband, Donald, for blessing me with the opportunity to live in beautiful Florence, Italy! Deep heartfelt thanks to Lisa Fugard for your careful editing commitment working with me through ten drafts to arrive at the final edit of *Carina*. Deep heartfelt thanks to the Biola University team overseeing The Malcolm Initiative (see biola.edu/malcolm-initiative) and for giving me guidance as to the publishing of *Carina*: thank you Barry Corey, President of Biola, Brian Shook, Ed Stetzer, David Horner, Scott Singletary, Grace Gluck (for your excellent copy editing) and Max Horton (for your brilliantly talented graphic design for the cover of *Carina* and chapter icons). Deep heartfelt thanks to my prayer partners Donald, Ruth Montzingo, Meredith Bernados, Mary Beth Minnis, Louise Duhamel, Celeste Bailey, Bev Siligmueller, and Vicki Rose. God bless you all!

Carina

Brookstone Publishing Group
An imprint of Iron Stream Media
100 Missionary Ridge
Birmingham, AL 35242
IronStreamMedia.com

Copyright © 2025 by Laura Eastman Malcolm

No part of this publication may be reproduced, stored in a retrieval system, or transmitted in any form or by any means—electronic, mechanical, photocopying, recording, or otherwise—without the prior written permission of the publisher.

Iron Stream Media serves its authors as they express their views, which may not express the views of the publisher.

Library of Congress Control Number: 2025903954

Psalm 23 is taken from The Authorized (King James) Version. Rights in the Authorized Version in the United Kingdom are vested in the Crown. Reproduced by permission of the Crown's patentee, Cambridge University Press

Luke 14:13 is taken from the Holy Bible, New International Version®, NIV®. Copyright © 1973, 1978, 1984, 2011 by Biblica, Inc.™ Used by permission of Zondervan. All rights reserved worldwide. www.zondervan.com. The "NIV" and "New International Version" are trademarks registered in the United States Patent and Trademark Office by Biblica, Inc.™

Front and back cover designs and chapter icons designed by Max Horton, Biola University

ISBN: 978-1-960814-16-6 (hardback)
ISBN: 978-1-960814-17-3 (ebook)

1 2 3 4 5—29 28 27 26 25

www.ingramcontent.com/pod-product-compliance
Lightning Source LLC
Chambersburg PA
CBHW050246010526
44107CB00003B/206